AS THE TWIG IS BENT, SO GROWS THE TREE

A Personal History of Medicine at Flinders

DAVID WATTCHOW

Wattchow, David (author)
As The Twig is Bent, So Grows The Tree
978-1-922890-26-9
Author Biographical | Personal History of Medicine at Flinders

Typeset Minion Pro 11/16

Cover and book design by Green Hill Publishing

These are my recollections of my time and experiences at Flinders University (School of Medicine) and Flinders Medical Centre (FMC). 'As the twig is bent, so grows the tree' is a proverb that refers to the shaping effects of early childhood, on personality and career. I have expanded its use here as I have detailed the influence of Flinders on my career, from my time as a neophyte student through to research training, specialist training and my life as a consultant surgeon. The memories are laced with humorous anecdotes along the way.

Dedicated

To the memory of Professors Gus Fraenkel, Jim Watts, Garry Kneebone and Lindon Wing, and to mark 50 years since the inaugural class of medical students.

Acknowledgements

My thanks go to Dr Neil McIntosh for early photos of
Flinders Medical Centre.

The sound editing advice and attention to detail by
Susan Polmear is appreciated.

Chapter 1

Beginnings

Flinders University and Flinders Medical Centre are named after the British navigator and explorer Matthew Flinders. At the age of 27, Captain Matthew Flinders commanded a leaky old vessel, the *HMAS Investigator*, from which he produced some of the most wonderfully detailed charts of the coastline of Australia. They are accurate to this day. He published a thesis titled, *A Voyage to Terra Australis*, from which Australia gets its name. It encapsulated a number of adventures and voyages, and he took seven years to write it, when he was imprisoned on Mauritius. It is said his wife put the published work in his hands on his death bed.

His was a life of discipline, youth and adventure – lessons for us all – but even this adventurer needed a mentor. In his case this role was filled by Sir Joseph Banks, who was on the ship *Endeavour* with Captain James Cook, and underwrote many voyages of exploration.

Bust of Matthew Flinders outside the Registry Building, Flinders University. Sculptor: John Dowie. This bust was unveiled by the Duke of Edinburgh in 1986 during his visit to the University, and a number of the alumni of the medical school attended. I remember that a marquee had been erected in the courtyard and John Brayley, who was later the State Chief Psychiatrist, was in attendance too.

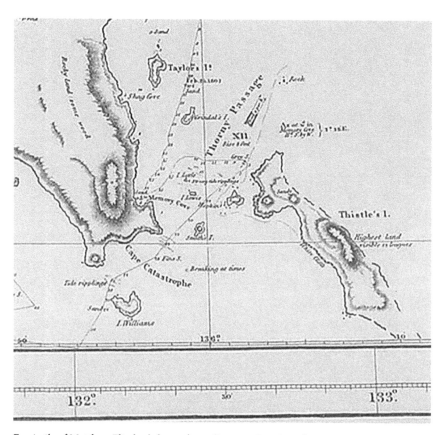

Facsimile of Matthew Flinders' chart of coastline near Port Lincoln.

Chapter 2

Student Days

In early 1974, a group of students assembled outside the Sports Centre. We were the inaugural class in Medicine at Flinders University. The University had begun as an offshoot of Adelaide University only 10 years earlier, and then assumed its own identity.

Setting up a medical course was the brainchild of **Peter Karmel**, the first Vice-Chancellor of Flinders University and a Professor of Education. Karmel's mantra was 'experiment and experiment boldly', and his legacy is perpetuated in the 'Karmel Endowment Fund' that supports research endeavours throughout the University.

DAVID WATTCHOW

Third year of Medicine.

Still, as 17-year-olds straight out of school, we did not know any of this. In the second year, when mature age students were accepted, they provided seniority and good balance to our obvious youth.

Much of the construction and ethos of the school was overseen by **Professor Gus Fraenkel**, but my earliest memories are of commencing studies 'up the hill' in the School of Biological Sciences. This was because at that stage the medical school was just a shell, still under construction.

Cartoon in the Medical Library foyer - Gus Fraenkel putting together the Medical School, and, dreaming of Oxford.

Gus Fraenkel

The hospital under construction. The medical school is built.

A young university, and the bare site of Flinders.

Early planning. University Vice-Chancellor Roger Russell, Premier Don Dunstan, CEO John Blandford, Dean Gus Fraenkel and Mrs Blewett (wife of the architect).

Like many courses of the day, our programme was a general introduction to Biology, Chemistry and Physics. We were lectured by **Jo Orbach** (Biology), **Professor Malcolm Thompson** (Chemistry) and **Professor Alex Hope** (Physics). I recollect practical classes where we distilled DNA and operated on rats for Neuroanatomy.

In second year, we made our way to the medical school, one step behind the builders. A medical library was constructed, along with an anatomy laboratory/museum and a series of cubicles adjacent to the library for student study. It was all new and exciting.

Professor Fraenkel espoused the links between research, teaching and clinical care. He was of German origin, educated in Oxford, spent time in Ontario, Hamilton, where he obtained the advanced model for Flinders, and Dunedin; and then he was head-hunted to Adelaide.

Really though, I am getting ahead of myself – the need for another major hospital in Adelaide, was perceived by the Government of the day,

Sir Thomas Playford was the Premier. It was a Liberal Government, but it changed to a Labor Government when Mr Donald Dunstan became Premier. I was later to learn that making decisions of this magnitude is what governments do best. Indeed, that is their role.

Construction started on the site of an old tuberculosis sanitorium. There are photographs of Mr Dunstan 'turning the first sod' astride a large Caterpillar tractor – just hidden behind him is the actual operator.

The Premier, Mr. Don Dunstan, turning the first sod.

It is teachers who make a medical school, not buildings. The novelty of this new medical school attracted people from all over the globe. I wonder if they knew what they were getting into? They came to southern Adelaide in remote South Australia from Europe, America and Africa.

Some of the early personalities were:

Professor Laurie Geffen: The first Professor of Physiology. His photograph depicts the intelligence of the man. He had worked around the world, including with the famous anthropologist Raymond Dart, of Rift Valley fame, and put on the curriculum *Introduction to the Study of Man*, by JZ Young. He was appointed to Adelaide University, but soon came to Flinders, where he established novel research work, including the development of immunohistochemistry, to view neurons that synthesised noradrenaline (using antibodies to Dopamine B Hydroxylase - in conjunction with Robert Rush). Using antibodies to visualise nerve cells and their chemistry was to become a major focus of the school. Ultimately, he changed direction, and went on to train in Psychiatry, and later became Dean of the Medical School at the University of Queensland.

Laurie Geffen, the first Professor of Physiology at Flinders.

Professor Andrew (Andy) Rogers: Professor of Anatomy. I remember how he tried to instill into us the principles of scientific investigation. He was using the technique of autoradiography, with chemicals tagged to radioactivity to visualise active cells.

He oversaw our introduction to Anatomy, where we commenced dissection of the human body, cadavers having been loaned by the Adelaide Medical School. The students were split into groups. The group I was with started dissecting the buttock, a rather fatty area, and looking for small cutaneous nerves, with very rudimentary tools indeed. We had a marvellous technician who assisted us, Carlos Kordjian. Along with another technician, Bruce Harper, Carlos produced some superb dissections that are preserved in the Anatomy Museum to this very day. They are as good as any I have ever seen, and in my opinion better than those in the Hunterian Museum in London. At the outset of our studies in Anatomy, we all purchased a real skeleton. Mine was definitely the skeleton of a woman, evident by the angle of the bones. She was in our study at home for many years, and was used by our daughters, Naomi and Kimberley, before she was finally donated to the Department of Anatomy.

Andy Rogers returned to the UK, and quite by happenstance I saw an obituary to him and his work in the *Journal of Anatomy*.

I was well into consultant years when the then Chair of Anatomy, Rainer Haberberger, asked me if I would be willing to support the purchase of an Anatomage table. This is a life-size computer reconstruction that can be 'dissected'. So, $10,000 later, the human body could be dissected without the smell of formalin!

Carlos Kordjian and Professor Andy Rogers: Photographs in the Anatomy Laboratory, FMC.

Bren Gannon: Bren seemed like an alternative character. He was appointed to the Department of Anatomy and had wide interests. He worked with Colin Carati from the Medical School. I recollect that he was involved with the Royal Australasian College of Surgeons (RACS) regarding the Anatomy curriculum and exams for surgeons. Bren was one of the contingent of staff independently recruited from the Department of Zoology at Melbourne University run by Geoff Burnstock (along with John Furness and Marcello Costa).

Saxon White: A punchy, rugby playing (Australian team) cardiovascular physiologist from the Eastern states.

Charles Straznicky: A quiet Hungarian embryologist. Embryology was always rather a mystery to me, but *Moore's Clinical Embryology*, a wonderful book with beautiful line drawings, helped. Charles did microdissections of tiny embryos.

George Wyburn: A Scottish Professor of Anatomy. He was small and his conduct instilled confidence in his use of all the formalin he had encountered. Both he and Charles expanded our perceptions of the world, especially with their accents.

Michael Berry: Professor Berry was a biochemist from New Zealand, and a friend of the ophthalmologist Fred Hollows. When working with Krebs in Oxford, he had pioneered a means of digesting the liver into its component cells, the liver being a biochemical factory. This one technique opened up the study of pathways and cycles of chemical pathways.

Michael Berry attracted some very talented biochemists:

Phillip Barter: Knowledgeable about lipid metabolism. With Phillip, I did a summer Scholarship spinning down plasma to isolate the lipid fractions.

Greg Barritt: Expert in Calcium metabolism.

We'd had a visit from the famous biochemist **Hans Krebs**, of the Krebs (glucose) cycle. He was Michael Berry's PhD supervisor in England, and when Michael introduced him, he became visibly emotional – this was a mark of his humanity.

The Famous Four: Laurie Geffen, John Chalmers, Michael Berry and Andy Rogers tucking into meat pies!

The Centre for Neuroscience

One of the unique developments of the school was the Centre for Neuroscience. This was the brainchild of **Professor Laurie Geffen** who was the founder of the Australian Neuroscience Society, at a meeting at Flinders in the early 1980s. Underpinning the Centre of Neuroscience at Flinders were a number of prominent scientists and clinicians. Some names come to mind, Marcello Costa, John Furness, Robert Rush, John Willoughby, Bill Blessing, John Chalmers. I will refer to both the scientists and the clinicians.

Marcello Costa: Costa is Italian. He has a medical degree from Turin. Apart from being a brilliant scientist, he was the brains behind many of the concepts and advances in the Centre. When he studied medicine in Turin, he was a student intern in Anatomy. This was where, a generation before, the Nobel Prize winners Rita Levi Montalcini, Salvador Luria and Renato Dulbecco had started. Costa worked with a number of famous scientists, before migrating from Italy to Melbourne, to work with Geoff Burnstock. There, he was chosen by Laurie Geffen as foundation Lecturer in Physiology. Costa is multitalented. He enjoys and plays music, loves literature, and engages in physical activities such as windsurfing and mountain climbing. He has discovered and named peaks in Patagonia. A lesson from this man is the value of being very widely read. For him, reading widely provided the ability to see and link matters in science, for instance, the perception that labelling a protein in the cerebellum (Spot 35) might also label intrinsic sensory neurons in the gut. He was experimenting with localising enteric neural pathways with wheat germ agglutinin before his protégé, Simon Brookes, developed a more accurate label (DiI). Marcello was Convener of the 'Centre of Neuroscience', and was President of the 'Australian Neuroscience Society'.

Professor John (Barton) Furness: An Australian with a Physics degree background, he was from Melbourne, where he was a PhD student of Geoff Burnstock. Together with Molly Holman, Burnstock was one of the founders of modern neuro-gastroenterology. Both were students of Edith Bulbring, a remarkable German refugee who was at Oxford, where she was the first to record smooth muscle electrophysiology. John changed his focus to the gut and the nerves within the gut wall that control its movements. He formed a formidable partnership with Marcello, and 'Costa and Furness' graced many seminal publications. He took on the Chair in Anatomy from Andrew Rogers, and eventually moved back to Melbourne University.

Robert Rush: An Australian, Rush was most interested in trophic factors that governed nerve growth. I remember one talk by him, about how he had treated a rat with a spinal cord injury with growth factors. After some weeks the animal was moving normally, whereas the control animal was still paralysed. This seemed to me to be the way of the future.

Many of these impressions of the enormous depth and breadth of our teachers were gained over time. As greenhorn students, we had little idea of the talents of these people. We were just imbibing what was known about the human body and how it worked. There were student gatherings, parties, football games, cricket matches, laughter and loves. It is little wonder that some of this group of students became prominent in medical research. I am sure we did not fully appreciate the central role of Gus Fraenkel. My first recorded memory of Gus is a photo taken in the old Lecture Theatre 4, with all of us about to enter the world of clinical medicine. Many have white coats but not necessarily ties.

Class of '79: First white coats, substantial hairstyles. Fourth Year Lecture Theatre 4.

Back row: *Helen Patroney, Gary Shanks, Julie Forsyth, Marion Catford, Craig Shearing, Mike Forster, Henry Duncan, Janet Nicholson, Taunton Southwood, Peter Ingham, Rob Pegram.*

Fourth row: *Phillipa Heard, Kingsley Wood, Suzy Szekely, David Luis, Sarah Mares, Kate Burgess, Geoff Seidel, Steven Deller, Steven Byrne, Diane Campbell, David Wattchow*

Third row: *Peter Papay, John Glastonbury, Arnold Seglenieks, Bernadette Skrebels, Paul Runge, Rob Van den Berg, David Kelly, Francis Makinson, Richard Watts, Deborah Pfeiffer, Robert McIver.*

Second Row: *Dorothy Jones, Wendy Graham, Jane Treadwell, Jane Hawkes, Michael Sandow, Jamie Cooper, Heather Waddy, Gregory Otto, David Sare, Christine Hilton.*

Front Row: *Valerie Summers, Lachlan Warren, Wajidi Kerni, Rupert Thorne, Gus Fraenkel, Diane Cassidy, Paul Duke, Chris Baggoley, Claude Wischik.*

The hospital opened for patients just ahead of the students. We had some very talented clinical teachers. Those that come to mind are:

John Chalmers: Professor Chalmers helped 'make' Flinders. He hailed from Sydney. He was an active Professor of Medicine, and seemed rather omniscient to us students. He truly espoused Gus Fraenkel's ideals. John was a superb clinician, heavily involved in research. He ran a lab of talented scientists and clinicians – Ida Llewellyn Smith, Leonard Arnolda, Jane Minson, Malcolm West - and attended the Neuroscience seminars. His main interest was the control of blood pressure, and this has a considerable neural basis. He was one-time Chair of the 'National Health and Medical Research Council' (NHMRC), and Dean of the Medical School. He retains a great fondness for Flinders and its graduates. His contribution is commemorated each year by a 'Chalmers Oration' at which a distinguished overseas visitor delivers an address. He was recognised nationally with the Companion of Australia (AC) award.

Richard Burns: A talented neurologist in the days before CT scanning. Richard Burns lent credence to Flinders Medical Centre, as he came from the Royal Adelaide Hospital (RAH). I well remember his demonstrations of neurological signs in patients, which I believe stemmed from his experiences in Queen's Square Hospital in London, along with his time in Cleveland, USA.

John Willoughby: Another talented neurologist and neuroscientist/researcher, who had a very logical way of examining the nervous system. He was interested in electrical signals generated by the brain (EEGs) and epilepsy. The electrical recordings may be confused with muscle activity, and for this reason, he recorded brain signals while paralysing the subject without sedation! He was Chair of the 'Centre for Neuroscience'.

Jim Watts: The first Professor of Surgery and one of the youngest Chairs of Surgery in the country. Jim Watts built up a very good and harmonious department. He was an excellent clinical scientist with an eye for asking relevant questions. He ran a number of clinical trials, a skill he no doubt acquired from the famous British surgeon John Goligher of Leeds. These studies included use of antibiotics for the prevention of surgical infection; intensive v. non-intensive follow-up after bowel cancer surgery, and, a randomised comparison of various forms of bariatric surgery. These studies remain relevant to the current day. He appointed a senior surgeon from the RAH – Allan Campbell. Many appointments flowed like that of Neil McIntosh. After his retirement as a surgeon, Watts established Fox Creek Wines, a very well-regarded winery in McLaren Vale.

Jim Watts, founding Professor of Surgery.

The first surgical staff at Flinders: Peter Slattery, Richard Hamilton, Jim Toouli (standing); Neil McIntosh (Chief Resident) and Jim Watts.

Neil McIntosh: First Chief Resident in Surgery. Neil McIntosh spent several years in the UK apprenticed to surgeons such as Savage and Tanner, and working impossibly hard, which he did all his life. He taught his protégés respect for tissues as well as the value of kindness. A very busy surgeon in private practice, he could always spare time for patients at FMC. He was a real example to us all.

John Hall: A Senior Surgical Registrar, his art was to challenge, his mastery was statistics. He was often to be found at night huddled over the computer seemingly relaxed and with a can of Coke. He became Editor of the *ANZ Journal of Surgery*.

Richard Southwood, Jo Sweeney and Colin Steele Scott: A group of academic and practical orthopaedic surgeons.

Richard Southwood: The first Chief of Orthopaedics, involved with scoliosis surgery (Harrington Rods) and bone lengthening. As well as assisting with those operations, I learnt plastering for fractures and reducing fractures from him. He was fond of surgical history and drew my attention to the work of Charnley, of hip prosthesis fame, and *Extensile Exposure* by AK Henry.

Jo Sweeney: A mild-mannered Senior Orthopaedic Surgeon who had seen and done it all. He had arms of steel from years of physical work with fractured bones.

Colin Steele Scott: I remember him, for two reasons. Firstly, he played the clarinet in clinics, it resonated rather well, and secondly, he was fond of saying, "If you go cutting for pain, you rarely find it!" Very true.

Garry Kneebone: Professor of Paediatrics and a natural raconteur. He was in demand for student events. You can see from this beautiful overleaf photograph of him examining a child that he obviously has the baby's trust. He had an interest in child nutrition and the treatment of obesity, which is currently a big problem.

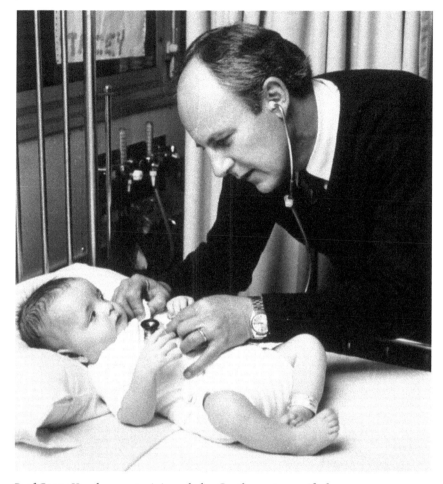

Prof Garry Kneebone examining a baby. Gentleness personified.

Ross Kalucy: Professor of Psychiatry and a trained physician. Professor Kalucy had an interest in eating disorders. He often took students under his wing. A rather enigmatic character, he did a nice analysis of the movie *Shine*, about David Helfgott. He had some very good staff. One doctor whom I remember was Sandy McFarlane, who developed a career around Post-Traumatic Stress Disorder. He gave us a marvellous lecture on suicide, and played *Candle in the Wind* by Elton John during that lecture. It was a moving experience. Kalucy completed his medical career with an interest and involvement in Acute Psychiatry.

Warren Jones: First Professor of Obstetrics and Gynaecology. Jones headed the first unit to achieve invitro fertilisation in South Australia. As a student, I found that being involved in childbirth was a fun time, but sometimes it involved very long hours. There was always a competition with the midwives to attend births. The Department is now quite large, and Obstetrics and Gynaecology has become quite sub-specialised. Professor Jones appointed good people, one of whom was Bob Bryce with whom I had the pleasure of working on the Clinicians' Special Purpose Fund (CSPF).

Dr Jones took on public causes in 'retirement'. One of these was a campaign to save the Repatriation General Hospital (RGH), which resulted in the reopening of that hospital.

Michael Cousins: First Professor of Anaesthesia, interested in regional anaesthesia and chronic pain. Professor Cousins performed anaesthesia for thoracic cases and familiarised students with the oesophageal stethoscope, by which means we could listen to the heart sounds and breathing at the same time. I had an earpiece fitted to the end, but I really couldn't discriminate that much! When he was President of the Pain Society, Cousins famously, met Pope John Paul 2.

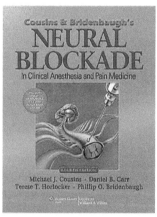

Michael Cousins, First Professor of Anaesthesia, and the book on Neural Blockade that he co-authored.

FLINDERSWEEK

No. 243   THE FLINDERS UNIVERSITY OF SOUTH AUSTRALIA   SEPTEMBER 14-20, 1987

A WORLD WITHOUT PAIN

A historic meeting took place recently when His Holiness Pope John Paul II received representatives from the International Association for the Study of Pain (IASP) and International Pain Foundation (IPF) at his summer palace in the hills overlooking Rome.

His Holiness Pope John Paul II greeting Professor Michael Cousins watched by Professor John Bonica (front), Emeritus Professor of Anesthesiology at the University of Washington, Past President of the IASP and Chairman of the IPF Advisory Board with Professor Ronald Melzack (rear), Professor of Psychology at McGill University and Immediate Past President of the IASP.

Among those present was the Professor of Anaesthesia and Intensive Care at Flinders, Michael Cousins, in his capacity as President of the IASP and a board member of the IPF.

The IPF is a non-profit organisation established last year by the IASP to promote public and professional education programmes about pain management.

The ultimate goal is contained in the words of Albert Schweitzer who once said, "We must all die. But that I can save (a person) from days of torture, that is what I feel as my great and ever new privilege. Pain is a more terrible lord of mankind than even death himself".

Chairman of the IPF Advisory Board, Emeritus Professor John Bonica, originally suggested that His Holiness be asked to support the IPF objective.

A private familial meeting was subsequently granted at which His Holiness spoke with each of the twelve people present before making an address dealing with his personal letter of support for the aims of the IPF.

The following Sunday during a service in public, His Holiness endorsed the work of the IASP and IPF and commented directly on the need for better pain research and improvement in the treatment of pain throughout the world.

The remarks were widely reported by the Italian press which was "extremely encouraging", said Professor Cousins.

Although he was unable to release any names, Professor Cousins said further assistance would be sought from other "world personages".

According to the IPF, freedom from pain should be a basic human right, "limited only by our knowledge to achieve it".

For example, cancer pain can be virtually abolished in up to ninety per cent of patients by the intelligent use of drugs.

However, the reality is that fewer than half those suffering cancer pain will obtain effective relief, even in societies with access to sophisticated modern medicine.

Fortunately that's not the case at Flinders where the Pain Management Unit has acquired an international reputation for the successful treatment of acute and cancer pain.

Establishing the "world class" facility was greatly assisted by the Flinders Medical Centre Volunteers who donated $100,000 to the Unit. Credit is also due to the South Australian Health Commission and the Minister for Health, Dr Cornwall, said Professor Cousins.

"I think they showed an enourmous foresight and an ability to look at a new area that badly needed attention."

For example, pain is often most poorly managed in those who are least able to help themselves —

the young and the elderly.

According to the IPF, children often receive little or no treatment, even for extremely severe pain, because of the myth that they are less sensitive to pain than adults and more likely to become addicted to pain medication.

In the elderly, pain is often dismissed as something to be expected and therefore tolerated.

People who suffer from severe or unrelenting pain often become depressed and may lose the will to live.

The IPF says part of the problem of poor pain management lies with health professionals who fail to administer adequate doses of opiate drugs to counter

pain of acute or cancerous origin.

There may also be a lack of awareness or skill in using various therapies or even in selecting the most appropriate treatment for specific pain conditions.

In certain circumstances pain may be seen as merely 'psychological' and effective medical aid withheld if the inevitable interplay between somatic and psychological aspects of pain is misunderstood.

Inadequate pain management would also be less common if patients demanded their basic human rights to be free from pain, says the IPF.

Another part of the problem in developing countries lies with the

Continued on page 2

Michael Cousins meets the Pope.

Morris Peacock: A thoracic surgeon and a very strong man physically, he did a lot of swimming, at 4.00 am! I went to his operating theatre to learn thoracic surgery and oesophagectomy. I was impressed that the list started on the dot of 8.00 am, and I remember that there was absolute quiet in the theatre and the phone was off the hook. I later employed this example of turning off all music and chatter in my own practice. He came to value his residents over time, and I learnt the elements of thoracic surgery such that I was able to do emergency surgery later in my career.

Garry Phillips: Professor of Anaesthesia in later times, but he had many roles in running the Emergency Department, in resuscitation courses, and setting up the ICU. I recollect that he was very keen on the development of protocols, like the insertion of chest drains - the argument being that this minimised errors. Later this approach was championed by Rob Padbury, Chief of Surgery.

Anthony Radford: Held the first Chair of General Practice. He had worked extensively in New Guinea, and he famously diagnosed his own aortic dissection and had it repaired successfully.

Dean Southgate: A 'salt of the earth' General Practitioner who ran a busy practice in Clovelly Park. I spent time in that practice, where we took our own x-rays, set fractures, and so on. It is uncommon for a GP to do that now.

Ian Moffat: A country GP from Karoonda, who ran the Emergency Department (ED) for quite some time.

Anthony Radford, Dean Southgate and Departmental Secretary, Pauline Bransden.

Early Teaching Staff

Back Row: *Michael Cousins, Terry Nicholas, Malcolm McKinnon, Malcolm West, Lindsay Barrat, Dean Southgate, Peter McDonald, John Bradley, Cyril Brown.*

Standing: *Elizabeth Cant, Graeme Barrow, Michael Berry, Richard Whitehead, Warren Jones, Garry Kneebone, Geoff Benness, Alec Morley, Pauline Hall, Charles Straznicky.*

Seated: *Phillip Barter, Russell Linke, Laurie Geffen, Gus Fraenkel, Jim Watts, Andy Rogers, Ross Harris.*

Ground Level: *Anthony Radford, Michael Sage, Saxon White, John Chalmers.*

John Bradley, Alec Morley and Peter Roberts-Thomson: A mix of talented immunologists and haematologists. Through them I was to see, from afar, huge advances in these fields in both understanding and treatments. In that era, acute leukaemia was a death sentence. One of the patients at this time was a young man with this disease and anorectal sepsis. The latter required a stoma formation. Years later he came back for a stoma reversal, and was 'as fit as a mallee bull'. He'd had modern treatment and bone marrow transplantation and was now getting on with life. I had expected he would be dead, and I think I remarked, "What are you doing here?" This field saw the implementation of new drugs, too, such as tyrosine kinase inhibitors that were effective against chronic myelogenous leukaemia, and GIST tumours.

I provided a service for lymph node biopsy to assist with lymphoma management. I would never delay the surgery, and placed patients on the earliest operating list available as they were always worried. The traditional approach then, was to treat the patients without necessarily explaining matters to them, but I found that stressed patients and families appreciated having information.

Peter Roberts-Thomson: Interested in patients with scleroderma, which is a difficult and debilitating illness. I remember that he detailed changes in the nail bed capillaries that denoted this condition.

Alex Gallus: Quite a superstar of medicine. He was an haematologist, and was involved in international trials on the prevention of venous thromboembolism, a major concern during surgery. He provided significant help in studies we did on the application of venous thromboembolism prophylaxis, by Clexane. He was a great example of how a good scientist is a good doctor; the thesis that good research underpins good clinical medicine was developed in an NHMRC report by Simon McKeon, Australian of the Year in 2011. As well as being a philosopher, Alex Gallus gave good basic medical advice. Many of our clinical conversations would end that way.

Doug Henderson: A pathologist, and a giant of a man physically and intellectually. Doug was integral in the establishment of the link between asbestos exposure and mesothelioma. I recall his booming lectures on pathology, and I particularly remember that he was involved in the shutting down of the asbestos mine in Wittenoom Gorge in Western Australia. His knowledge was encyclopaedic and his pathology reports were essays. For all of Doug's professional prestige, I found him most approachable, and in later years he became a good colleague.

Radiology

The Radiology Department was initially headed up by **Geoff Benness**. Some talented folk joined that Department:

Mick Sage, who secured the first CT scanner in the State.
Allan Wycherley, who headed Nuclear Medicine.
Marc Agzarian, **John Slavotinek** and **Peter Downey**.

We were involved in the research side as well. I did a summer project with **Dr Phillip Barter** on lipoprotein metabolism. I acquired an appreciation of the types of lipoproteins and their metabolism, and gained an insight into a research laboratory and how it functioned.

These were very talented people, but what really characterised their teaching was a strong personal interest in the students and delivering the best teaching possible.

Given this vast array of talent and teaching, what became of us all? I focus on a photograph taken at the graduation of the final class, it shows that 42 doctors graduated out of an initial class of 64. I don't think this could have been anticipated from the outset, and it makes me wonder about the selection of students. Of course, students change and develop, some gravitate to different fields, while others have their initial choices confirmed. Many became practitioners of medicine and there have been countless outstanding careers amongst the graduates.

Here we are at graduation outside the lecture theatres.

Back row, left to right:

Peter Ingham: A successful ophthalmologist

Geoff Seidel: Psychiatrist, geriatrician

Greg Otto: Surgeon, RACS Head, South Australia

Deborah Blood: Psychiatrist

Richard Watts: GP became an anaesthetist

Tauny Southwood: Professor of Paediatrics (Rheumatology), Birmingham, UK

Rupert Thorne: GP, Gawler, South Australia

Jamie Cooper: Head of ICU, Alfred Hospital, Melbourne; undertook several major studies on treatment of severe brain injury; awarded AO

John Glastonbury: Ophthalmologist, Queensland

Mike Forster: GP, Hamilton, Victoria

Di Campbell: A South Australian

Robert Van Den Burgh: Physician, rheumatology. Head of Medicine Noarlunga, Southern Adelaide Local Health Network (SALHN)

Gary Shanks: GP; involved in the Sydney-Hobart Yacht Race disaster

David Wattchow: I didn't have any other tie except that floral one!

Lachlan Warren: GP, became a dermatologist; Head of Dermatology, Women's and Children's Hospital, Adelaide

Paul Runge: An American, returned to the USA; ophthalmologist

Steve Deller: GP

Robert Pegram: GP, National Head of General Practice (Commonwealth postion)

Kate Burgess: Prominent in Aboriginal and Women's Health, Sydney

Kingsley Wood: GP, psychiatry

Peter Papay: Psychiatrist

Rob Gribble: Liaison Psychiatrist, Alfred Hospital, Sydney

Here we are at graduation outside the lecture theatres.

Middle Row:

Arnold Seglenieks: GP, became a surgeon; marvellous artist; Millicent, South Australia, and New England

Chris Baggoley: Many roles; ultimately Chief Medical Officer of Australia; awarded AO

Dorothy Jones: GP

Jenny Wood: GP

Val Luckman (then Summers): GP, Noarlunga Emergency Department

Helen Patroney: GP and Surgical Assistant in Bariatrics

Julie Forsyth: Ran a busy multidoctor general practice in Marden

Suzy Szekeley: Anaesthetist

David Sare: GP; devised the 'black cross' markers of road fatalities around the State when in Millicent; he is now at Byron Bay

Front Row:

Steve Byrne: GP, Goolwa

Heather Waddy: Neurologist

Mike Sandow: Orthopaedic surgeon; specialised in shoulder problems

Claude Wischik: Became Professor of Neurophysiology, Cambridge, UK; explored treatments for Alzheimer's disease; moved to Scotland

Paul Duke: Dentist, oral surgeon

Deborah Pfeiffer: GP, then involved in breast cancer screening

Robert McIver: GP, Family Relations

Marion Catford (then Drennan): Psychiatrist

Absent from this photograph are:

Wendy Graham: Anaesthetist, Germany

David Kelly: Psychiatrist

Craig Shearing: A South Australian

When I was an intern, I found surgery fairly boring, especially being the assistant. I had been a keen amateur fisherman and it struck me that the bulky knots being used to tie the nylon suture for abdominal closure could be replaced by knots used by fisherman to tie nylon. My suggestion became adapted as the 'Half Blood Knot'. Professor Watts promulgated the method and wrote it up in the *British Journal of Surgery*. It attracted commentary in the *British Medical Journal*, and once, I was quizzed about it by a Senior Surgeon in the changeroom at Royal Adelaide Hospital!

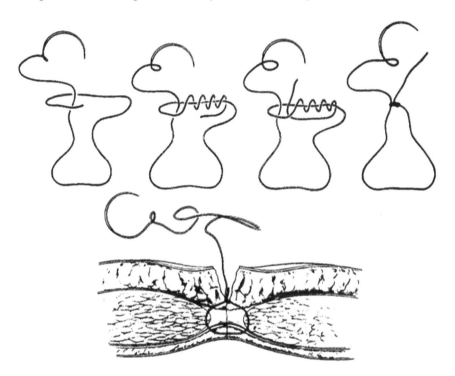

Drawing of the half blood knot as published in 1984. For tying nylon in abdominal closure.

In our year we had a very strong and fit man, Henry Duncan, who was on the national scull team of eight and was rowing for the Olympics. He was shown considerable latitude, and took the year off. They won the race in Moscow. Now he is a urologist.

At the end of the course, Gus Fraenkel decided there would be a qualifying ceremony and prizes. These traditions have endured. On the basis of examination, I was awarded prizes in Medicine, Surgery and General Practice. I remember aspects of those exams. In Medicine, I had a patient with the lateral medullary syndrome, which is a pattern of midbrain damage due to stroke. I was probably lucky to have seem a case before. In Surgery, I was asked how to set up a Thomas Splint. As it was, Thomas was a distant relative, as told by my proud Grandmother. The Medicine Prize at that time was a text on the history of medicine by Lyons and Petrucelli. On the cover was a painting of a seminal event in medicine.

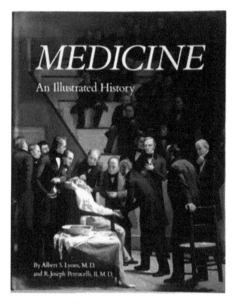

Prize for Medicine.

The front cover shows a painting of the first ether anaesthetic in the Ether Dome, Boston, Massachusetts, given by Dr T Morton, who was a dentist.

As we progressed through Medical School, the hospital grew. I well remember going to see the very first patient admitted. We were in attendance for the first patients coming into the Emergency Department, which was then located in the chapel due to an oversight by the planners. One of the early cases was a patient with a fractured tibia, evaluated by **Dr McIntosh**. I was amazed at the matter-of-fact way he dealt with the problem.

Dr McIntosh taught us the fundamentals of surgery. One day he took us to see a patient with pressure sores. The patient had just died, he didn't tell us and I thought the nurses were being a bit rough with this old lady.

All the clinicians were good teachers, and they accepted teaching as part of their positions. After all, they were taught gratis and were doing the same for us. That is what was done.

I recollect my attachment to the Obstetrics area. The midwives were not particularly welcoming to medical students, and I think some of this tricky relationship may persist to this day. We had to attend a full labour, and for my first I had a woman delivering her first baby. In other words, it took a long time. Her husband came in and went to sleep in the corner while I held her hand. Still, I was mentioned in the birth notice. I was savaged by the ward nurse in charge of obstetrics because I was not wearing a tie. I am not sure if I even had a tie by fourth year, but I soon bought one! Gynaecologists and urologists famously wore bow ties, as ordinary ties would get in the way of examinations.

When we were students, the course was intensely evaluated. When we were being examined in Anatomy, one station was surface anatomy and for this the 18 year-old daughter of one of the professors attended, clad in a bikini. Various embarrassing questions were asked. Judiciously, this would not be allowed now.

Another memorable term was in Psychiatry, which we did at Glenside Hospital with its magnificent old building. We were somewhat wary of the psych patients as the hospital took the criminally insane, so we teamed up for reassurance. We played footy with the patients and enjoyed the grounds.

A famous book published at that time was *The House of God* by Samuel Shem, and it related to his experiences training as an intern at the Beth Israel Hospital in Boston. It was rather dark, but the lesson I gained from reading it, was that a callow intern often learned the medical ropes the hard way. More fun, and sarcastic, was the *Doctor in the House* series by Richard Gordon in the UK. It was almost trumped by *Yes Minister*, when the Minister visited a new hospital without any patients, which was true of Flinders at one stage!

Quite a talented medical student band was formed. It was called Zona Pellucida, which is the name of the layer around a developing embryo. Helen Patroney was the lead singer and other members were Rob Pegram, Peter Ingham, Geoff Seidel, both on guitars, Tauny Southwood, drums, Arnold Seglenieks and Deborah Blood. They played at a number of student gatherings.

We formed a running group around the ovals and university. Jamie Cooper, Tauny Southwood and I would head off for a run after study. I only had Dunlop Volleys, which were rudimentary sandshoes. Later, I competed over a similar route for the Corporate Cup, representing our lab.

We didn't have a lot to do with the uni 'up the hill'. There was an excellent record society in the Undercroft, now demolished. For a peppercorn membership we could borrow real records with associated scratches, and thus I sampled a broad spectrum of music from classical to pop. Popular bands at the time were Led Zeppelin, Fleetwood Mac and the Eagles; Carole King and Linda Ronstadt were at the height of their performances.

In our senior student years, we delved into some quite advanced medicine. During a term in Intensive Care, I undertook a medical retrieval to the Riverland in a Royal Flying Doctor plane to pick up a young man with a severe head injury. We conducted autopsies, not many are done now. On one occasion I was left doing an autopsy on a complex medical case when the whole ward round and Senior Consultant turned up to see the findings, as the pathologist had left for the day.

We had rotations at the Repatriation General Hospital at Daw Park, which was largely occupied by old Diggers (veterans). As well as fascinating pathology, they had great stories to tell if you took the time to listen. I saw an old man with many scars and learned that he had been shot and left for dead on the Kokoda Track. Now, he thought that was fair enough, but he remembered too, that the opposition soldiers came and urinated on him. He rallied, returned to Australia, and went back.

On another occasion, I was to operate on a big man, and I commented to him, "This will match the scar on your opposite chest." "Oh, that was where I was bayoneted before I clobbered the bloke with my sharpened spade," he replied.

Everybody from our graduation class has had a great career and not wasted their education. Who could have predicted this from the outset, for a group of 17-year-olds fresh out of school? Bright people were chosen, educated well and motivated well, and the rest is history. These basic elements will never change.

Undoubtedly, my group of students had a real bond. Years later, I was on sabbatical in the UK and visited Cambridge. While walking along the Backs near the River Cam, with a view over to the famous colleges, I bumped into Claude Wischik and his family, and Claude and I recognised each other straight away.

At the completion of my student days, I was privileged to be awarded the University Medal for the top graduate. The medal has an inscription showing the Greek god Prometheus on it. He was the man god who brought the gift of knowledge from the gods to mankind.

Lessons:

People make an institution like Flinders Medical School. They may come from all over the world.

Buildings help.

Take a talented group of students from high school, educate and motivate them well, and they will do well.

The University Medal depicting the Greek god Prometheus bringing the gift of knowledge to mankind.

Aerial photograph of the Hospital and Medical School and the University, showing the co-location of the two - the brainchild of Gus Fraenkel (insert).

Flinders University and Medical Centre

Chapter 3

Junior Doctor Days

After my student days I took the customary pathway of internship. This is a probationary period where you are closely observed, but with increasing autonomy and authority to order tests and prescribe. Those were busy days. I was often on call for 36 hours straight. I quickly learned to cut to the chase, I could no longer take the exhaustive histories and examinations that were done during our student days.

On those long shifts, we often gathered after midnight for something to eat, which was provided free of charge. There was a late-night cook called Efram, who made excellent toasted sandwiches. Fortunately, those long shifts don't occur anymore where we experienced considerable tiredness. Less fortunately, the toasted sandwiches and late-night camaraderie have also disappeared.

As interns, our first paid job, we were paid $4.12 per hour, which was less than what the cleaners received, not that we minded, as we were finally getting some real pay.

The first group of interns, Flinders Medical Centre. This photograph from 1980 is largely unchanged from student days, but with a few new people who had come along.

It was always a strange atmosphere at night. It was dark and the bays were lit by single lights. The corridors were long and dark too. It felt rather eerie. Sometimes we would see in the dawn, with the sun rising over the ovals and playing fields.

One of our early lessons was to treat colleagues or their relatives as normal patients. One classmate's son fell from a bike. The boy complained of a headache, so I organised a skull x-ray, and it showed a depressed fracture that required surgery. Another child was complaining of pain following a cycle accident, and this time an x-ray showed a fractured femur. This taught me the value of an independent evaluation when a family member is concerned.

One day while I was doing a spell on Orthopaedics, Dr Southwood said he was off to 'the Adelaide'. I assumed a busy chap like him was also working at the Royal Adelaide Hospital. In fact, he was off to the Royal Adelaide Golf Club!

During that period, I recall winding out a leg lengthening apparatus on a child and Harrington Rods procedures (for scoliosis). Venous thrombosis was common but hard to diagnose post bone surgery and it could be fatal.

In the 'old' ED, there were two sides, A (serious cases) and B (minor cases). In the early hours it was sometimes quite quiet, so we would play cricket with a drip board as a bat, and a rolled-up ball made of Sleek, a bandage.

Towards the end of internship, there is a choice to be made. Many of us, including me, chose physician training. We were probably influenced by the excellent physicians of the day, such as Professor Chalmers. We needed to experience the broad church of medicine before we made up our minds. Some of us changed direction. **Chris Baggoley** went into the evolving specialty of Emergency Medicine, and gradually I changed to Surgery.

Why? After a year of being a Resident Medical Officer (RMO), I still hankered after cutting and sewing. This key practical skill is what defines a surgeon. Maybe it came from my grandfathers, one was a carpenter and the other a farmer. As a student, I soaked up books on practical surgery, and I was happiest in the ED sewing up lacerations, which we were allowed to do.

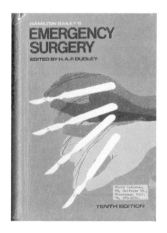 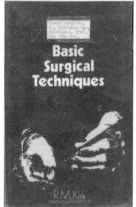

Surgical texts of the day.

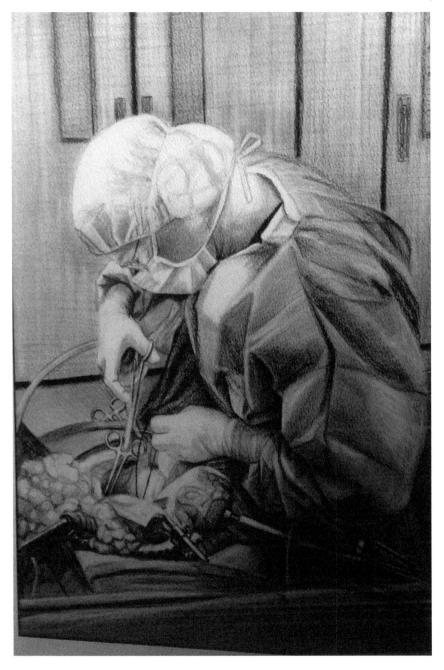

A charcoal drawing of David Wattchow suturing in the abdomen by Avril Thomas, Artist.

We acted as shepherds for candidates being examined for their Fellowship exams. Once, during the Fellow of Royal Australasian College of Physicians (FRACP) exams, a senior physician asked the candidate to demonstrate the apex beat of a patient. The candidate confidently placed it in the left chest, the usual location of the heart. Without batting an eyelid, the examiner failed the candidate, as the patient had dextrocardia and the apex beat was on the right. Years later, I operated on cases where there was situs inversus in the abdomen, it was most odd, with the liver on the left and spleen on the right.

We had surgery-wide seminars in the Horseshoe Seminar Room when Professor Watts was in charge. On one occasion, a case was being presented of a fractured hip in a very ill older person. Professor Watts, who was often dozing, questioned the need for any surgery at all. The cocky Senior Registrar said, "Of course, and who are you?" Professor Watts' reply was fantastic, "Watts, James Watts - like James Bond."

Once, Jim Watts invited the Professor of Surgery at Adelaide, **Glyn Jamieson**, to come and help with a young man with portal hypertension. He was a most impressive man with beetling eyebrows that were instantly recognisable. It was a good lesson in the importance of calling for help from a person with particular expertise.

I first heard **Professor Jamieson** enunciate Hanlon's Razor: "When you suspect malice, it is usually incompetence." Followed by, "They will reinvent the laparotomy sooner or later."

I considered studying Neurosurgery for a while. I was quite interested in head injuries and their management. One needs the support of good mentors at such a critical time, however, and I did not have that in neurosurgery.

I didn't make that choice again, and applied for General Surgery. Somehow, I managed to get through the rather frightening interview, which was conducted at the Royal Adelaide Hospital. There was a long wooden table surrounded by august surgeons, and I was an outsider from Flinders. But the person chairing the interview was **Robert Britton Jones**, a surgeon, who was a kind man. He put me at ease, saying, "We are here to help." I remember a particular question, "When are you getting married?" I'll never know how I came up with the answer, "When I find the right girl, Sir." It must have convinced the panel, as I was accepted to train as a surgeon. That question would not be asked these days.

The other time I experienced kindness from the RAH surgeons was when I was attending a conference, and at breakfast a senior surgeon, **James Young**, asked me to join him. I later experienced his good and encouraging nature on a number of occasions.

Another senior registrar was a Scotsman with a sense of humour. He was exceeding the speed limit when coming into the hospital and a police car pulled up alongside. Quick as a flash, he waved his stethoscope at the window. The police officer responded by waving his handcuffs.

Whilst a registrar, I had a funny incident where a nurse had marked in the patient's chart 'has passed an offensive stool'. Upon seeing this, the prickly consultant remarked, "Since when is a stool not offensive?"

Once, I had occasion to be thankful for the presence of a really big policeman. I had an odious patient in the ED who was sparking off, and the police were called. A huge policeman filled the doorway and immediately the offender quietened. Not a word was spoken. This was in the days prior to Ice.

In the early 1980s, general surgery was truly that – dealing with hand injuries, head injuries, as well as the general run of abdominal pains and emergencies. There were some very good registrars to help and instruct us. **Jim Burnett**, **Paul Jury**, **John Hall** come to mind. Plus, there was always the bible, the reference to check, *Hamilton Bailey's Emergency Surgery*. These were exciting times. Appendicitis was a teething ground and there was dealing with trauma and various gut perforations. They were long days and nights, but were usually buoyed up by the work at hand. Gus Fraenkel had written a small monograph titled, *A guide to house surgeons in the surgical unit*. It was a bible of distilled wisdom, and is still germane today.

An event, when running in the Belair Park, resulted in me fracturing my wrist when attempting to hurdle a chain across the track. I broke the distal radius and had a plaster put on. I couldn't do anything, and took it off after a week. I shouldn't have as it was rather painful. At varying times, I have cut my chin, broken ribs, gone over the handlebars of the bike... just the cost of doing business. When I was on the receiving end, I was sharply reminded that we all may require medical care.

One very important lesson was not to get too far ahead of yourself. One night, I was sewing up facial wounds on a young woman, and the senior nurse was peering over my shoulder, "Should you be doing that?" she asked. You can learn a lot from the nurses. Often an experienced theatre nurse will tell you what to do, or simply slap the relevant instrument in your hand! Never ignore it when theatre nurses say the count of packs is incorrect. I often disbelieved them, but a search always showed a blood-soaked pack tucked up by the spleen or in the pelvis. Any embarrassment is usually salved by the relief at not creating a surgical disaster.

Receiving an award: Professor Marshall, Davis and Geck representative, Heather Dooley and David Wattchow.

I had rotations at various Adelaide hospitals. When at the RAH, I was called by a medical registrar to see a skin lesion on the left forehead of a patient admitted with a stroke. The patient could not speak, and his right side was paralysed, which was indicative of left brain hemisphere damage. On looking at the 'lesion', I could discern grey matter of the brain. I suggested a skull x-ray, and it showed a bullet in the left brain. The man had been shot.

Dealing with famous personalities and egos was not easy. Some were terrifying. A surgeon had just arrived from the UK and we were doing a cholecystectomy for his first case. At that time, a glass syringe was used for the contrast injection into the bile duct, and during the surgery, this rolled off and smashed to smithereens. The surgeon became well established, though, and had a penchant for student teaching.

You hadn't completed a term at a teaching hospital unless you were subject to criticism from a prickly consultant. I was organising a surgical list at the RAH and had to organise equipment for an operation. I really had no idea, so made a best guess and organised a particular surgical stapler – the wrong one!. That was embarrassing. There was the famous vascular surgeon **Justin Miller**, who amongst other things, invented the gortex patch to prevent neointimal hyperplasia in femoro popliteal grafts. Years later, I heard the 'Miller Patch' presented in London, it was the same person. He was obtuse but inventive. A certain degree of creativity leads to advances. An example being, when Warren and Marshall discovered the role of Helicobacter in peptic ulcers, it was after Dr Marshall famously drank a broth of Helicobacter and developed an ulcer as proof.

We did everything in the early days. When I was a junior registrar at FMC, a patient came in having put a chainsaw through the back of his leg. I had the anatomy book open for that one. It was *Grant's Atlas,* as I recollect, a marvellous publication of 'real' dissections and anatomy.

One of the last cases I helped manage as a registrar was a chap who had swallowed a rolled-up raincoat for a drinking bet. It proceeded to unfurl in his stomach. Attempts at endoscopic removal were fruitless, so he required a laparotomy. I can still see an image of **David Hill** withdrawing the raincoat like a magician! Other interesting foreign bodies were placed up the rectum. One was a garlic bottle that perforated the sigmoid colon; the pathologist reported 'cholesterol free' garlic. Another chap placed a bottle of Lynx deodorant into his rectum. I could only get a purchase on it with a toothed Kocher's forceps, and upon withdrawal it perforated the container, spraying me with Lynx. That was hard to explain.

Professor Paul O'Brien was one of the chief abdominal surgeons in Flinders at the time. He had research interests in the area of peptic ulcers, which was to become transformed by the advent of proton pump inhibitors and the discovery of the role of Helicobacter. I was his junior registrar. One day he said, "David, it's time you did a PhD." He had spoken to John Furness in Physiology/Anatomy, and persuaded me to apply for a scholarship from the RACS, 'The John Loewenthal Scholarship', which I obtained. I was underway. This underscores the importance of a good mentor who gives support and sees the way forward.

I therefore transitioned into the lab for a while, but I still acted as a registrar and did private assisting. I kept my hand in.

Lessons:

Immerse yourself in the study of medicine. It is a long apprenticeship.
If you want to specialise in surgery, do a few other things first, don't be in a hurry.

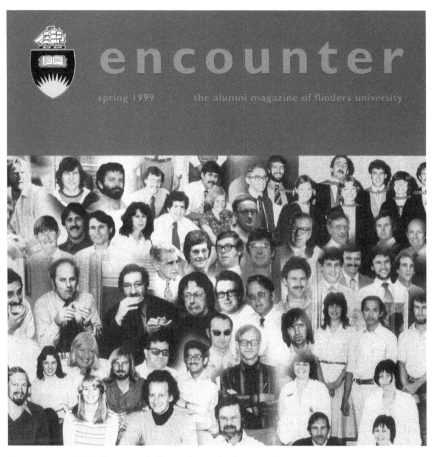

*A montage of Flinders people from the early days, in **Encounter** magazine.*

Chapter 4

PhD Studies

I commenced PhD studies in 1985. To me, the world of science and investigation was challenging and quite different from the world of clinical medicine. My broad premise was to investigate the human enteric nervous system utilising the techniques developed by Marcello Costa and John Furness, and colleagues. There were plenty of staff and resources, but there was no set timetable of what to do. There was a lot of reading to do, and no computers. There was a library of Index Medicus, where medical and scientific papers could be searched. Luckily, there were a few publications on the human gut. I think Professor O'Brien thought I might 'solve' the big clinical problem of paralytic ileus, but that was to come much later.

I did have access to the operating theatres, however, and was permitted to take specimens of human intestine. This is a foreign environment to most scientists, and an intimidating one, but for me it was home territory. The juxtaposition of the clinical world (theatres) with the labs is really what Gus Fraenkel had in mind.

I have an early memory of when I had finally produced a slide of the gut, albeit with much help, and was trying to work the intricacies of a fluorescence microscope, whereby a wavelength of light excites a chemical, thus bouncing back at a different frequency. At last, I could see something glowing and I was sure it was nerve cells. A bewhiskered chap with a floral shirt was in the microscope facility. I later learned that he was none other than **Ian Gibbins**, a super-intelligent scientist who had come from Melbourne Zoology to join Furness and Costa's labs as a post-doctorate. He went on to become the Chair of Anatomy. He had a look down the microscope and gently informed me I was looking at red blood corpuscles. Boy, I had a lot to learn. Surely, I should be taking out appendices.

Fortunately, matters improved but it took many months. I have often observed similar experiences for clinicians who have come to the lab. The process is one of immersion and osmosis, combined with curiosity and some intelligence.

I surveyed the whole human gut, with sections stained with antisera to the known peptide markers. At that juncture there were no good antisera to the commonest neuro-transmitters acetylcholine and noradrenaline. Whole mounts of the gut nervous system were being done on small animals with thinner intestines, but not the thick, ropy, auto-fluorescent human intestine. My observations led to a number of publications in the top journals of the day. Right there and then, I had no notion that I was doing something special in a world-wide sense.

I well remember sending my first manuscript to John Furness, rather proud of myself. It came back covered in red ink. This was another humbling experience. After graduating in medicine and broadly training in surgery, I thought that I could write, but clearly not. While I was initially dismayed at John's numerous red jottings, I soon realised I was fortunate to have such feedback. This was the start of another learning process, on how to actually write scientifically – how to analyse and discuss data, how to look for flaws, how to limit speculation. They were all skills that could be applied broadly.

I never really thought of funding as an issue. I gained a National Health and Medical Research Council scholarship, a princely sum of

$11,000 per year. I had no family responsibilities and just needed the odd meal and money to fuel the car for bushwalking trips even though I was aware that other students, especially those with young families, were doing it tougher.

There were some issues regarding authorship of papers that required some personal courage. Nowadays, the NHMRC has strict author guidelines. Back then, all images were captured on film. We developed our own films and printed the images in a darkroom. Further education, in which I was ably instructed by Janet Keast, was shading out undesirable bits of dirt/dust on the image!

My thesis, 'The Distributions of Peptide-containing Nerve Fibres in the Human Gastrointestinal Tract in Health and Disease', was taking shape when word processing had just arrived. At that time, floppy disks were used to load processing programmes onto the computer. The floppy disks (they don't exist now, fortunately) were removed, the work was entered and saved on the computer. The work should always have been backed up to make a second copy, but I did not and had my whole literature review on one disk. That review just disappeared one evening! I realised this with horror and I felt thoroughly beaten up. Thankfully, **Roger Murphy,** senior scientist, was able to find it, for which I was extremely grateful. Back up everything was the lesson learned!

Roger saved my bacon again, when the final printing of the thesis was done. I have the ability to inadvertently crash a computer system, and at this critical time, the whole thing went down. Roger rigged a cable from the one functioning computer to the one operational printer and it was produced, along with precious photo images.

Technology was to further let me down. Photocopiers that assembled large documents had just come in. Hooray! The copier produced the six copies of my thesis for assessment. Only days before getting on a plane to the UK to resume training in surgery, my wife, Margaret, discovered that the new gadget had inserted a series of pages back to front. This was in the car on the way to the only binder that was open in a hot Adelaide

January. Everything was reassembled on the side of the road, and it was bound correctly.

The thesis was forwarded to examiners overseas and was passed and later, I was to meet some of those examiners. It's a big job to properly study a thesis. I have assessed a number and I have always tried to remember the blood, sweat and tears that have been shed in their production, while offering constructive criticism.

For a clinician, one of the unstated benefits of doing a PhD is that you are a much freer agent. You might step out of the operating theatre and hospital and find a big wide world out there. I was always keen on bushwalking and the simplicity of travel it afforded, and that was how I met Margaret. After a whirlwind courtship of some months, we boarded a plane to the UK.

Other benefits were that I was free to train in upper and lower gastro-intestinal endoscopy. **Derwin Williams**, a very patient physician, trained me. There were no video scopes at that time. Any dual training was with a split lens, but this diminished what the operator viewed. He must have had great tolerance as I struggled through those scopes.

I did quite a lot of surgery on call, and assisting. At one stretch I had the second busiest log book in the State. At a PhD interview, this drew comment from **Professor Jamieson**, Chief of Surgery at the Adelaide Hospital. He was concerned that it might impede my studies, fortunately I was able to complete the doctorate satisfactorily.

I met many talented people while doing the PhD. Apart from John Furness and Marcello Costa, there were the senior scientists allied with the Department. These included:

Ian Gibbins: Became Professor of Anatomy
Judy Morris: A Research Fellow of the NHMRC
Ida Llewellyn Smith: A top electron microscopist
Joel Bornstein: Now a Professor in Melbourne
Penny Steele: First to successfully label neurons with the synthetic enzyme for acetylcholine

Jim Galligan: American, heads up a large lab in the USA; editor of a major motility journal.

There were my fellow PhD students, such as **Janet Keast** who is now a Professor at Melbourne University. We were supported by a host of technical staff with **Pat Vilimas**, **Sue Graham** and **Janine Edwards** coming to mind. In recent times **Nan Chen**, **Adam Humenick** and **Melinda Kyloh** have provided excellent support. It was a very fertile environment in which to be.

I had the temerity to send a manuscript to the famous *New England Journal of Medicine* (NEJM) in Massachusetts. We had found a marked reduction in vasoactive intestinal peptide in nerve fibres in cystic fibrosis samples, and thought this might be important. Regrettably, this view wasn't shared by the reviewers and I think the manuscript was on the next plane back from the USA.

At that time, it was not common for surgeons to embark on a PhD but since then a link has been drawn between research and being a good clinician. This was the subject of a report by Simon McKeon, Australian of the Year in 2011.

Lessons:

There is a big world out there full of talented people. They are more than willing to encourage and help.

Professors Simon Brookes and Marcello Costa.

Chapter 5

Back to Registrar Days

In 1988, I moved to be a junior registrar at the Royal United Hospital in the city of Bath, UK. I was joining a line of illustrious trainee surgeons. It was a special time, being the first year of married life. Margaret and I lived on site and worked hard, but we had two out of three weekends off and used those to explore the country.

Australians are well trained and much sought after by the British and I learned a lot from the experience. I had a tough introduction, however, as the handover was done by a **Dr Tony Holbrook** who 'had done 'undreds of cases'. How was I going to get by, I wondered? Fortunately, my training in Australia held me in good stead.

One humorous anecdote was when I was doing a clinic and outpatient surgery in Warminster, a town near Bath. I followed **Robin Smith** (aka Smithy), who was in his Saab. I was in the dilapidated old Fiat that was passed on from the prior registrar and I had the accelerator pedal flat to the floor all the way, to keep up with him. We arrived and Smithy said, "You're doing the list!" The first case was a man for a vasectomy. It was cold, being the middle of winter, and the theatre nurse poured a litre of ice-cold Betadine, an antiseptic, into the patient's groin. Needless to say, the testicles retracted to somewhere up around the patient's ears. Thus, the vasectomy was 'interesting'. Out of respect for the patient, I retained focus and composure.

My life as a registrar in the UK involved a lot of night work and emergency cases. The first night, when I arrived at the flat, Margaret was waiting up for me with a cup of tea. The next time when I returned quite late, she was awake but in bed. Eventually, the lights were out and just a mumble came from the bed.

"What's that smell?"

"That is the combination of rubber gloves and faeces."

"Can you get rid of it?"

"No."

One evening in Bath, a patient presented with an ischaemic lower limb due to an embolus. I pulled out the embolus from the femoral artery with a Fogarty catheter (Fogarty was a medical student). For this bit of plumbing, I was paid one pound, but if you called on the Bath plumbing service out of hours, the fees were sixty pounds per hour!

The UK is delightfully different and it takes a while to get used to the country. Even two hundred years after settlement by the English, Australians were still viewed as colonial cousins. We weren't bad at cricket though, and I employed my beach cricketing skills to effect in the Bath versus Bristol Hospitals cricket match. The game was played on the Lansdowne Oval, which backed onto the hospital and had a great backdrop of the Beckford Tower. It is said that the famous West Indian batsman, Sir Viv Richards was 'discovered' on this oval, and that he hit balls through the hospital windows.

My moment of cricketing fame came when my consultant, Robin Smith, didn't want to go on the field. As we were about the same size, he loaned me his whites. I was called upon to bowl as a last resort. I put all my effort into that first ball and clean bowled the number one Bristol batsman. Shortly after that, I put down an off spinner that took the edge of the number three bat and was snicked to the slips. Bristol was in disarray and quick wickets followed. That performance is remembered to this very day.

While at Bath I was involved with a young patient with severe appendicitis. He developed postoperative hyponatraemia (low sodium level). It took a long time to twig to the diagnosis of adrenal infarction (Addisonian crisis). The Senior House Officer (SHO) pointed out to me that the patient was on the Waterhouse Ward. Sir Rupert Waterhouse no less, the Waterhouse of the Waterhouse/Freidrickson Syndrome of adrenal infarction.

The English have a unique sense of humour. It was traditional to stop for coffee mid-morning, and the Senior Health Officer (SHO) would bring it to the group. One day a mug full of coffee was cracked and it spilled all over **Simon Gregg-Smith**, the SHO, and a little splashed on Mr Robin Smith's shoe. In an even tone he said, "Simon, it's my day in the Bath Clinic today, and there's coffee on my shoe." Whereupon Simon, himself covered in steaming coffee, took out his handkerchief and cleaned Mr Smith's shoe.

Simon had his revenge. There was a good view of the carpark from the hospital. Simon obtained a Jaguar car and parked it alongside Mr Andrew Turnbull's Jaguar (one of the consultants). He remarked on this at morning tea, without identifying himself as the owner. So, we all trooped down to look, whereupon Simon proudly announced it was his.

The English were quite fond of 'chip butties' and occasionally 'sausage butties'. After one of either of these, there was no need to eat for the rest of the day.

Margaret and I visited London on a number of occasions as it was only a short train journey. On a particular trip I met one of my PhD assessors, **Dr Ted Howard**. On another occasion we caught up with a classmate, Heather Waddy, and stayed with her in Mecklenburg House on Russell Square. We stayed there on subsequent occasions and it was a haven, particularly the year when we had just returned from travels in Ireland and Margaret and our daughter, Naomi, were both sick with gastroenteritis.

Twenty registrars from Adelaide went to Bath before European working directives put a stop to the rotation. When Robin Smith died prematurely of a ruptured cerebral aneurysm, a plaque in his memory was erected by the Aussie registrars in the Royal United Hospital. We were united in our appreciation and sorrow at his passing.

Lesson:

It's a long road, enjoy the journey.

The author alongside the plaque for Robin Smith in Bath, UK.

Chapter 6

Back to Australia

After a year it was time to return home - home to final exams in Surgery. These are seminal exams and they set a standard for surgical practice in Australia. This standard is maintained by the Royal Australasian College of Surgeons (RACS). It is through this accreditation that patients can be assured of skill and expertise in the surgical procedures they undergo. The exams loom as a big event for students, and they are. I would judge the effort required to prepare for the exams as similar to producing a thesis.

All students have their exam stories. To this very day I can remember the cases I was asked to assess. They included a huge thyroid mass, a trans-axillary sympathectomy (a small scar that is difficult to see in an Aboriginal patient), and breast cancer spread to the spleen (very rare). I was passed a liver and asked to describe the segments, and promptly dropped it. Next, I was passed a box of gloves. The one I took out was actually on the bottom, so all the gloves came out! At least that lightened the atmosphere.

The examiners must have been in a friendly mood, as I passed. I took a sherry with the examiners in Macquarie Street in Sydney, and came back home as a Fellow of the Royal Australasian College of Surgeons. I was greatly aided in passing these exams by two Senior Registrars from NSW, **Phil Jeans** and **John Gani**.

While I was in Sydney, I took the opportunity of attending a performance of *Giselle* at the Opera House. I remember staying in a 'B and B' in Glebe, which was a welcome break from the intensity of the exams, although I completely lost my appetite with the stress of things. It was a half-hour walk to the Royal Prince Alfred Hospital (RPA) where the exams were being held. To this day I retain a fondness for the RPA.

I returned to life as a registrar and handled a vast array of cases but one in particular sticks in my mind. It was another night of sleeping at the hospital when a call came through, regarding a young lad with a head injury. He was unconscious and brought in by his worried mother. He had hit his head on the side of a swimming pool earlier that day, so there had been a lucid interval. The mother had rung the GP, who advised aspirin for the headache.

I went down to the Emergency Department and saw the boy, who was unconscious. One pupil was dilated, which is a cardinal sign of intracranial haemorrhage. So, without scans, which could be quite delayed as CT scanning was very new, I called for neurosurgical help and took him straight to the operating theatre. With shaking hands, I drilled into the temporal bone of the skull on the side of the injury. To my enormous relief, I encountered an extradural haemorrhage due to a lacerated middle meningeal artery. By now, the consultant, **Dr Reilly**, had arrived and we enlarged the bony cut, controlled the vessel, and packed him off to ICU.

Next day on rounds, we found him awake. On the TV screen in the room was footage of the space shuttle Challenger blowing up over Florida. Some things are unforgettable.

Years later, I met a strapping young man and his mother at a local church. "Do you remember operating on my son years ago?" she asked me. It is not possible to achieve such a happy outcome for all patients, an encounter such as this means the world to surgeons and their medical team.

A scanned letter from the child and parents. It was worthwhile doing all that training!

There were many long nights during that period. It was work all day, then all night, then all the next day, every fourth night! Happily, this would not be allowed any more. The one thing that helped us through the night was that after midnight the hospital restaurant opened with an onsite cook. When there was a big case at night, three or four hours into it I would jest with my registrars, "It's a bacon and eggs case." Nothing else cuts the mustard for energy.

We covered the hospital for anything surgical. This included working with children, and I was to learn some intricacies of childhood management that then applied to adults. We generally had good support from the consultants, but not always.

There were lighter moments. Once, anaesthetic registrar **Dave Bullen** and I did an 'art tour' of the hospital. We looked at and analysed the various artworks, largely prints, scattered around the hospital.

In 1989, I became the Chief Resident in Surgery at Flinders. This is an administrative role, but at that time it also involved counselling and cautioning. I shadowed **Dr Richard Sarre**, who was the best trained colorectal surgeon of the day. I learned a lot from him and later visited his mentors and teachers in the USA. I remember seeing the first patient treated for severe inflammatory bowel disease with a big dose of steroids. He had a central line placed for total parenteral nutrition (TPN), and a chest x-ray was taken to check it. The x-ray showed gas under the diaphragm from a gut perforation, but he was asymptomatic! This just shows the importance of checking up on results.

Lesson:

Work hard, and you will be rewarded.

Chapter 7

Life as a Consultant

Attaining a consultant role is a precarious time, and more than ever one relies on the help of mentors. In my case this person was **Professor Jim Toouli**, who took over from **Paul O'Brien**. He was my clinical PhD supervisor. I am sure others were involved, such as **Professor Villis Marshall**, who was the second Chair of Surgery after Prof Watts. The decision to appoint to a consultancy could only be made on the promise or likelihood of making some enduring contribution.

It is not possible to ever be ready for life as a consultant. Despite all the training, I felt the stress of knowing that now 'the buck stops here'. In a place like Flinders there are many colleagues who are very willing to help, and never refuse to do so. On some occasions, all anyone needs is a kind word from someone senior.

I did many things clinically, but on one memorable night I dealt with two infarcted (dead) stomachs in the chest, in a row. I have never heard of the same since. One of these was my first solo thoracotomy. I said to my senior colleague, Dr McIntosh, "I'm not sure I can handle this consultant business." He reassured me, "David, you're doing okay." It was a great example of moral support.

Medicine changes and advances over time. One thing is certain, it won't stay the same as when you started. Subspecialisation was one of the biggest impacts for me, and I perceived it hospital-wide. As a trained general surgeon, I did everything from the oesophagus to the anus, although at that time liver and pancreas surgery were specialised. I gradually focused on bowel surgery, and since the colon is a harbinger of disease, I was never short of operations to do. I retained a practice in splenectomy/node biopsy for haematological problems.

One of the big advances was in the treatment of peptic ulcer disease. The discovery of new powerful antacid drugs, the role of helicobacter infection (I actually heard the Nobel Laureate Robin Warren speak about his discovery), and advances in endoscopic treatment all came during my career. It made the need for ulcer surgery very infrequent. Even though we dealt with a perforated or bleeding ulcer on just about every on-call period in the early days this changed to be occasional surgery needed to put a stitch in a hosing vessel.

Another big change was the development of laparoscopy for abdominal surgery, which lessened the size of incisions. This proved to be especially valuable for operations on the upper aspects of the abdomen, such as cholecystectomy and fundoplication. I well remember tying the instruments together with rubber bands! For colonic operations, there was less proven benefit from laparoscopy, and, there was the sacrifice of touch and feel. I did not embrace this form of surgery. I was rather fond of saying I adopted the SLICE approach, Single Larger Incision Cost-Effective Surgery.

I did adopt laparoscopic technique for removal of a normal-sized spleen, in patients with immune thrombocytopaenic purpura who had not responded to any other treatment. **Dr David Watson** came from Adelaide Uni to instruct me on this operation. A key point was to place the patient left side up before mobilising the spleen. It often took as long to crush the spleen up and remove it bit by bit. We even tackled patients with a platelet count as low as one, who were at high risk of bleeding.

I retained an interest in splenectomy and was referred patients with very large spleens for removal, usually due to myelofibrosis and consuming various aspects of the blood. I found that a midline laparotomy and use of the Rochard retractor proved to be helpful, along with early ligation of the artery and vein in the lesser sac. Once these were secure, it was easier to free the spleen from the front and remove it with a flourish.

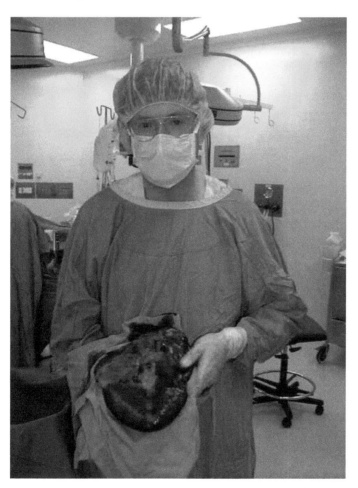

A giant spleen, weighing over 5 kg!

Sometimes the tail of the pancreas had to be removed to safely accomplish the operation. Out towards the end of the pancreas the duct was small, so I oversewed it with non-digestible nylon. From time to time it leaked and a pancreatic fistula formed, heralded by fluid in the drain left for this possibility. The advent of endoscopic retrograde cholangiopancreatography (ERCP) and pancreatic duct stenting magically dried up these fistulas.

I accumulated cases of intestinal malrotation, sometimes in patients who had undergone surgery in other hospitals. In dealing with these, I firstly consulted my paediatric colleagues as they saw more cases than I did. Generally, the large bowel had not rotated properly to the right side so that the small intestine was on the right and the caecum in the left upper quadrant. This predisposed to small bowel twisting and ischaemia. The operation devised to deal with this was called Ladd's procedure, it involved splitting the mesentery down to the vessels and then allowing the resultant adhesions to secure the bowel. This managed the risk of twisting, but not the motility problems that were present, so it was variably successful.

Through my specialty interest, I had many cases of rectal prolapse. The patients treated were predominantly elderly women, often with faecal incontinence. By and large, I dealt with these by a Delorme procedure, which involves inducing the prolapse and dissecting off the mucosa, thus leaving a muscle tube that is plicated back into the pelvis. By doing this in the prone position and using the anal Bookwalter for retraction, it was much easier. It could even be repeated if need be, and was essentially a day case surgery. Sphincter injuries were common and I would add a sphincter repair when required.

Nowadays, there is a plethora of options for this condition, and anal sphincter repair has fallen out of favour. A decent overlapping repair done prone, covered with a temporary loop colostomy, yielded good results. It was definitely required for childbirth trauma, which was severe and shattered the sphincter mechanism.

I was fortunate enough to observe the first liver transplant carried out at Flinders Medical Centre, by Dr Padbury. What most impressed me was the retraction system - Rochard retractor, which I later employed for abdominal surgery, as well as the Bookwalter retractor. This idea arose when I was operating late one night, at the suggestion of a theatre nurse, **Lyndal Klei**, who had seen it used by the vascular surgeons. I even rang Dr Bookwalter when I was visiting the Cleveland Clinic in North America, expressed my appreciation of his retractor, and had a chat. He put me onto his video of various forms of retraction systems.

Other advances that have occurred during my time as a surgeon have been screening for disease and detection at an asymptomatic phase (cervical, bowel and breast cancer) and advances in immunologic management (for example, in Crohn's disease, rheumatology). Most of all, were the advances in imaging. I remember when **Dr Michael Sage** introduced the first CT scanner to South Australia. It was incredibly slow compared to the modern versions, but it was a quantum leap in imaging. We were all amazed when Prof Watts scanned an abdomen to see the pancreas. There was a great photograph on the wall in the Radiology Department of Dr Hounsfield, from Cambridge, who invented CT scanning. The units of pixilation on such scans are known as Hounsfield Units.

All hospitals were thankful for a marked reduction in severe road trauma in this period. The introduction of seat belts, improved car design and better policing resulted in fewer deaths, from the 1980s.

Just about every field of medicine evolved and changed. There were huge changes in cardiology with stents, powerful antiplatelet agents; haematology with cases of lymphoma and leukaemia cured by chemotherapy and bone marrow transplantation; flexible endoscopic examination of the gastrointestinal tract and bladder; radiotherapy, which melted away some rectal cancers such that destructive surgery was not required; anaesthesia and pain relief, which were vastly improved. And, that's just some of them.

From the 1980s, another improvement with far-reaching consequences was the emergence of palliative care as a specialty. This was championed by Professor Ian Maddocks, Nobel Laureate. Prior to that, we palliated the patients as best we could on the wards.

It became routine to biopsy the small intestine from the first part of the duodenum, to look for a condition called coeliac disease. I discovered several cases amongst my patients. This condition is due to an allergy to wheat protein (gluten) and is treated by avoiding foods with that ingredient. These patients have a heightened risk of lymphoma of the intestines and I saw several such cases. An interesting link is that this was described by Dr Gough, a physician in Bath, where I worked as a registrar.

New diseases came along too. Around 1995, I saw a young man with anorectal sepsis who looked incredibly unwell. HIV had only just been recognised, and he had the disease. Nowadays, it responds well to antiviral treatments.

Screening for common diseases such as breast and colon cancer became routine during my time, having really kicked off with cervical cancer screening. This led to a shift in the stage of disease presenting, and a consequent improvement in the number of survivals.

One was always encountering unfamiliar cases. I was operating on a femoral hernia acutely, which seemed rather thickened. I took all the thick tissue out and opened it up, only to see half the appendix inside, aka de Garengoet's hernia! Likewise, one evening I was treating a patient on the ward with a bowel obstruction. This patient was listed for surgery the next day for a presumed colon cancer. The patient had developed acute limb ischaemia due to an embolus, but I could not feel the pulse in the other groin because there was a mass, a femoral hernia. So, I fixed both.

Cases of occult gastrointestinal haemorrhage were really tough. Usually, bleeding was from the stomach or duodenum or colon. Professor Fraenkel had detailed that the natural history of diverticular bleeding was to stop. Occasionally, it was from the small intestine, due to jejunal diverticulosis and vascular malformations. This would involve careful inspection and sometimes examination with an endoscope passed into the intestine via enterotomy. Normally, a bleeding area could be localised so it could be resected and the patient's life saved.

Surgery undertaken on colleagues would put one on one's mettle. There was an event where I was referred a senior staff member with bowel cancer. The surgery was straightforward but the pressure intense, as I had the Chief Anaesthetist and senior nurses present. The patient remains alive and well to this day and has led a full life. I later operated on a senior physician with bowel cancer. He appreciated my professionalism and my personal concern. He too, remains alive and well. At the end of the day, both were just ordinary folk, and they took matters in their stride.

Some tests of personal ethics came along. The appointment of new staff to positions of significance took much time and care. Many hours were spent reading and reflecting on applications with the aim of arriving at the best and most equitable outcomes.

Now and again, I encountered patients who were unequivocal in their requests of how I should treat them, sometimes these were startling. They ranged from alcohol and cannabis to Lethobarb, a product used in veterinary science. I would treat such wishes as diplomatically as possible, but firmly nonetheless.

One head, two arms, three haemorrhoids made the point about the anatomy of haemorrhoids.

Trauma cases are constant. The hospital would organise itself to deal with multiple casualties in a 'mass casualty incident'. I partook in several of these and ended up coordinating, and ordering senior surgeons around! Lessons would be learned. A major one was how quickly we would run out of supplies. We reviewed all the major trauma cases too, and I was the surgical representative for many years on this committee.

Akin to that was involvement with Root Cause Analysis, which was a committee set up to investigate when matters had not gone well. This was a broader effort in the hospital.

> *The only evidence of life is change.*
> – Ancient Greek saying, Heraclitus

Lesson:

It takes time to assume seniority. Don't expect it too soon.

Chapter 8

Continuing Research and the Gus Fraenkel Ideal

When I had passed the exams, and been appointed, I rekindled my links with the neuroscience lab. I was drawn to resume activity with the science group, which was unusual to do for a surgeon.

John Furness had left, but a young (about my age), bright Englishman, Simon Brookes, had joined the lab to work with Marcello Costa, who had a worldwide reputation. Simon was developing retrograde tracing of enteric neurons and had discovered that by applying the chemical DiI to the terminal branches of the nerve cells, it would be retrogradely transported back to the cell body over a number of days. It involved the invention of an organotypic culture apparatus to keep the tissues alive while this occurred. The dissections of whole mounts of intestine, and fluorescence microscopy, were by then established.

I soon set up a collaboration with Simon, and we set about performing retrograde tracing on samples of human intestine. I would do the operations, take a sample and go to the lab. We initially treated the human intestine like guinea pig intestine, applying tiny amounts of tracer. It was to no avail. On the verge of giving up, we crushed a glass slide, soaked it in DiI, applied the shards to the circular muscle of the gut, and to our great excitement saw a glowing motor neuron some days later!

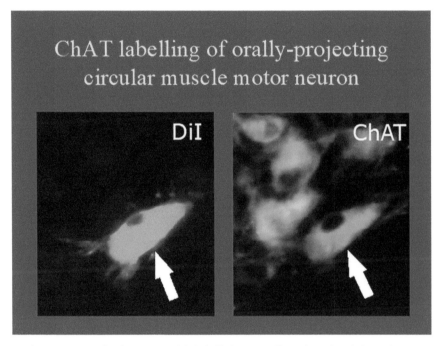

A photomicrograph of a retrogradely labelled nerve cell combined with histochemistry in the human intestine.

For me coming from the clinical world, this would simply not have been possible straight away. It required a fusion of clinical and scientific worlds. It was an example of what is now popularly known as 'translation', but then that word was not in our lexicon. No doubt the physical proximity of operating theatres to labs was significant - I have seen similar endeavours fail due to physical separation. Most important was the engendered closeness of interested persons. There are few places in the world with this physical setup and the desire for collaboration.

I set about mapping the distribution of human enteric neurons. Simon had invented a computer recording of mapping coordinates. This was hard work as it was all accomplished after I had done the surgeries and removed the pieces of human intestine. Of course, it involved a rigorous ethical approval process, and the development of safe means of dealing with potentially infectious samples. One would never knowingly use a sample from a patient with HIV or Hepatitis C infection.

Human intestine is not easy with which to deal. It does not easily peel apart, like animal intestine. It has generally been working for 70 years or more and is full of autofluorescence. To separate the layers requires sharp microdissection. When this was combined with the knowledge of anatomy that in the colon the longitudinal muscles are grouped into taeniae, with the area in between much thinner, it was possible to create whole mounts.

This research project led to a seminal publication on the technique and mapping that has formed the basis for ongoing work. It has rarely been repeated in the world outside our far-flung state of South Australia. One needs resources, one needs people, but most of all one needs ideas and energy.

Was all this work worth the effort? I was managing a career in surgery and nurturing a young family (with my wife, of course) along with the research work. I think that not one of these was possible without the other. History will be the judge.

The old recovery ward, FMC Active surgery and research.

Lesson:

Combining clinical work with science can lead to real advances.

Chapter 9

PhD Students

There is a developing thesis that good research underpins good clinical work. This was enunciated by Simon McKeon, Australian of the Year in 2011, in a report on Medical Research in Australia.

I might have been the first surgical PhD student at Flinders, but I was certainly not the last, **Drs Rob Padbury** then **Dr Lilian Kow** are surgeons who have completed a PhD in the lab. One of the advantages of clinical work is that you come across some talented trainees. In general conversation the subject of research might arise, and the trainee becomes interested in following your model. They might want to be like you, or aspire to a position in a public hospital and recognise that a research degree is a good stepping stone.

Thus, **Dr Anthony Porter**, who was a registrar on our unit, came and commenced a PhD with Simon and me. It was a good period, as he rapidly learned the techniques and combined retrograde tracing with neurochemistry. As it happened, a marker of cholinergic neurons had become available (antibodies to the synthetic enzyme, choline acetyl transferase, ChAT). Anthony was bright, and did a lot of good work during his candidature. Towards the end he branched out to label myenteric neurons from the submucosa. Like many clinicians, he recommenced clinical training before submitting his thesis so it was harder to complete the thesis. He must have developed a penchant for microdissection, as he became a plastic surgeon.

The next student under our guidance was **Dr Elisabeth Murphy**, a trainee. We had always struggled with proper quantification of neuron subclasses. Marcello Costa had come across a label to Hu protein, which labelled only cell bodies and not the confusing array of nerve processes. This really formed the basis of proper quantification of classes of neurons in the human intestine. By now we had a marker to nitric oxide synthase, which marks the major inhibitory class of nerve cells, as well as ChAT.

A puzzling clinical scenario is that of severe constipation. It is a condition which largely affects young women, and occasionally necessitates a total colectomy to relieve the symptoms. This gives abundant intestine to study. Dr Porter had found some abnormalities in the excitatory peptides in circular muscle, but this was only partial. These cases are only a few per year and tend to be referred to a major hospital like FMC. Dr Murphy defined a reduction in the cholinergic neurons in the removed colon, the inhibitory class (NOS) were unchanged. She has become a senior surgeon at the Lyell McEwin hospital, with an interest in research.

Dr Dayan DeFontgalland was working on our unit, and I well remember enquiring one day in the tea room whether he was interested in a PhD. "Yes," he replied. It always takes a while to settle on an area of unique study, and it is not initially clear. Simon Brookes was embarking upon studying the nerves extrinsic to the intestinal wall, that run from the spinal cord to the gut and influence its overall activity by synapsing on the enteric neurons. These nerves are in the mesentery of the intestines. In the guinea pig, the mesentery is a diaphanous membrane with the vessels and nerves clearly visible. Not so in humans, even in the thinnest person these vessels are buried in fat. This was another example of how hard human samples can be, but

Dayan set about dissecting these nerves and defining their chemical populations.

Moreover, he studied samples from patients with inflammatory bowel disease and defined an increase in the tachykinin populations of nerve fibres. He did some nice functional work too.

Around this time a bright young science student, **Simona Carbone**, commenced PhD studies, largely with Simon. She was to define the mechanisms underlying 'warmup', or restoration of physical activity in the intestines once removed from the animal. As part of her work, she undertook studies of functional activation of nerve pathways in human intestine. Simon had by now developed a device to stretch the gut wall and elicit reflex behaviour. This did not work well in human samples, so he and Simona resorted to electrical stimulation. By now, we knew that there was one population of ascending nerves in the gut wall, compared to several populations descending. Simona activated ascending nerves with electricity and to demonstrate nerve activity used blockers of neural activity. A confounding factor was that the gut is spontaneously active, but Simon found a statistical way of analysing it.

Thesis completion is a massive effort and ultimately has to be done by oneself, even with the best support in the world.

By now, my trainees such as Dayan DeFontgalland were generating the interest of students in their own right. This is how **Dr T Sia**, an energetic young man, came to join the group and commence a PhD with **Dr Nicholas Spencer** and me. Nick had just joined the group, he was a scientist from the famous Melbourne group via the USA, Dr Kent Sanders from Reno. Nick was interested in further defining the role of 5 hydroxytryptamine (5HT) in gut neurotransmission. The bulk of this chemical is found in the cells of the mucosa. Dr Sia was involved in this work, utilising immunohistochemistry and functional experiments on animal intestine. Sia was a surgical trainee who was dedicated to his PhD studies. He did night work in the ICU as well, and the lab staff famously bought him a pillow for when he dozed on his desk!

Part of Sia's work was studying whole animal colon in an organ bath. One would think that the human colon was far too big for any organ bath experiment. Dr Spencer had other ideas. Here, the essential role of the Biomedical Engineering Department came in. Under the influence of Nick, these engineers built a giant organ bath to house a whole human colon. Sia was involved in commencing studies on the contractile patterns of segments of whole human colon. This included studying samples from colectomies for severe constipation, and they seemed to be contracting fine after warmup. We didn't understand what this meant, but it was to be clarified later.

Like all the others, Sia assisted me in the private hospital. Everybody learned a lot there, and it was a good chance to review research progress.

Dr Phillip Dinning joined the group. He is a senior scientist from NSW, and Simon Brookes had seen his recordings of detailed colonic activity using a fibreoptic manometer. We managed to attract him to Flinders, and he was involved in further supervising PhD students **Dr Reizal Rosli**, a surgical trainee and **Dr Paul Heitmann**, who examined aspects of colonic motility contributing to faecal incontinence.

Dr Smolilo commenced PhD studies, looking at the chemistry of nerve interconnections in the enteric nervous system, (ENS) which was now possible with the resolution of confocal light microscopy. He has continued with a career combining research, surgical assisting, and a young family.

Dr Dominic Parker completed a Master of Surgery with the lab. It was in the area of sympathetic innervation of the gut, which underpins states such as ileus and constipation. He used confocal microscopy to assess the proximity of TH reactive fibres to various classes of myenteric neurons.

I had higher degree students in other areas too. **Dr Paul Hollington** examined homeotic genes in colon cancer in conjunction with **Dr Wayne Tilley** and **Dr Nicholas Rieger** did a detailed study of anal sphincter damage due to childbirth. Both have gone on to senior roles in the South Australian Health Service.

I guided, mentored and supervised eleven higher degree students overall. This is a very high number for a staff surgeon, and I am very proud of each one of them.

All of this work was underpinned by the talented laboratory staff. In the early days, **Pat Vilimas** and **Sue Graham** helped out with tissue sectioning and antibodies. **Janine Falconer** was involved with the human side of things for a while and **Nan Chen** and **Adam Humenick** greatly expanded our knowledge of the human gut and enteric neurons.

Lesson:

Encourage young talent.

PhD students: Anthony Porter, Elizabeth Murphy, Simona Carbone, Paul Heitmann, Reizal Rhosli, Tiong Sia, Dayan DeFontgalland, David Smolilo

Chapter 10

Students from across the Sea

We had a number of bright medical students who came from Holland, **Meike Berghuis**, **Ilse Hofmeester**, **Margreet Saunders**, **Elspeth DeVries**, **Merel Kuizinga** and **Rachel Moddejonge**. They were pupils of **Dr Vincent Niewenjhuis**, who was a Senior Registrar on our surgical unit (hepatobiliary). He had enjoyed his time in Adelaide - all the overseas trainees did, invariably living close to the beach. He set up the liaison with our medicos and the lab for the students to come.

I was initially approached by Meike about doing a research project with our group during her medical studies. "Sure," I said, and thought not much more about it until I was up in Simon's lab one hot summer's day and Meike appeared at the door! Hmm, one should plan these things better.

The students from overseas immersed themselves in the lab, and in Australian life in general. One of the best pieces of work was done by **Merel Kuizinga** on functional studies of human intestine. As part of resections for cancer of the right colon, a segment of terminal ileum is removed. The small intestine has simpler activity patterns than the colon and propels chiefly liquid content. We had organ baths for the specimens, detailed recordings, plenty of surgeries, and someone interested in doing the work. To get real insights as to what to do, we needed none other than Marcello Costa, who worked out how to vary the volume of fluid infused to stimulate activity, and how to block it using lignocaine. Nick Spencer was involved too. It seemed we were doing a right colon (and terminal ileal) resection every week! Merel produced wonderful work, which was published in the *American Journal of Physiology*, a top-flight journal.

Lesson:

There is a big world of talented folk out there.

Chapter 11

'Translating' Ideas into Clinical Applications

Apart from the intrinsic value of the knowledge, one really hopes for some application of research to the treatment of patients. This implies a knowledge of where the clinical problems are, and some appreciation of basic science knowledge and how this may be used.

My first example stems from our observation of a marked reduction in cholinergic neurons in cases of severe constipation. I knew it was possible to increase acetylcholine at neuromuscular junctions by cholinesterase inhibitors. The drug pyridostigmine does this as it was used to treat myasthenia gravis – this came from med student days. We set about using it to treat patients with constipation. It was quite ineffective. A different clinical problem is treated by cholinesterase inhibitors, and that is pseudoobstruction of the intestines, usually emanating from some other stimulus such as hip surgery; neostigmine is the drug used. This usually resolves when the primary problem settles, but not always. Recurrent pseudoobstruction can be difficult to treat. Using a cholinesterase inhibitor such as pyridostigmine proved effective. This just shows the circuitous pathway of clinical advances.

This was a rather imperfect study. The world of reviews for a clinical study is an exacting one and it is hard to get an idea published. Ultimately though, a committed, and bright RMO, **Dr Chloe O'Dea**, assembled the case series and put the work into publishable form. Such dedication is a hallmark of quality in general. She later trained in breast/endocrine surgery and was appointed to the consultant staff.

A *bête noir* of clinical studies is the randomised controlled trial. This method can only really be applied where there is doubt as to the better of two treatments. As Prof Watts had shown, intensive investigation of bowel cancer cases after treatment produced no survival benefit. Remembering that our clinics were very busy seeing these postsurgical cases, I wondered if follow-up by the patient's GP might be just as effective as a specialist review. I had collaboration with **David Weller** in the Department of General Practice at the time, so we devised a study, submitted it for national funding, and I thought no more of it.

The NHMRC provided no funding for our work on bowel motility. Indeed, the overall success rate is only about 8% and that is for top calibre researchers. I was feeling a bit flattened by yet another rejection when Dr Weller rang to say that we had been funded for the GP and surgeon study. I was gob-smacked.

Now the process of employing staff began. We had a really talented nurse, **Kelly McGorm**, who drove the study and obtained help from other states to increase the size of the study. When Dr Weller took up a Professorship in Edinburgh, Scotland he handed over the reins to **Professor Louis Pilotto**, then Chair of General Practice, and **Dr Adrian Estermann**, a talented statistician. Kelly left too, so we interviewed, and employed a marine biologist, **Zoe Hammett**. When Zoe went overseas with her family, I had to call her in England to obtain the passwords to unlock the computer that had the data! This is called doing it the hard way.

We were recruiting centres for a trial, to increase the size of the study. David Weller, Kelly McGorm and I were at Monash Medical Centre in Melbourne. Our football team, the Crows, was doing quite well at the time and I made lighthearted reference to its success. I had under-estimated the passions surrounding football, and one of the audience members went bright red with rage, as the Victorians weren't doing so well. We did recruit, however, from that centre!

After nine years from inception, we finally published the results of that trial in the *British Journal of Cancer*. In essence we showed equivalence for the modes of follow-up, although the GPs were better at doing the tests. There is a huge focus on follow-up still, with more, and detailed, testing, and to date it still has not shown any advantage. That study has been repeated in various guises over the last 25 years and the result is the same, so I was pleased to see our results standing up so well.

One would think I would know better than to embark upon another Randomised Controlled Trial. Again, it was due to chance events. Marcello Costa had seen a publication on preventing the arrest of gut motility that occurs postoperatively. He had passed the article on to Liz Murphy, who in turn sent it on to me. The article was by Dr Bauer of Pittsburgh, North America. It basically showed that in rats, handling of the gut induced activation of macrophages in the gut wall, and they in turn released prostaglandins that inhibited gut motility. Furthermore, by inhibiting prostaglandin production (by a Cyclooxygenase 2 inhibitor – not a COX inhibitor), the inhibition of gut motility was blocked - in rats!

COX (cyclooxygenase) 2 inhibitors (celecoxib and valdecoxib) were just making their way into clinical practice at this stage. The adverse cardiac effects were not yet known. I devised a clinical study of treating patients three ways placebo; standard COX inhibitor (Diclofenac); and COX 2 inhibitor (Celecoxib). I was by then a busy surgeon at FMC but even so, enrolling adequate numbers of patients was not easy. We gathered all the clinical data pertaining to gut recovery and side effects. Dayan DeFontgalland was working with me, and he was most helpful in the recruitment of patients. Approximately halfway through, the story about Valdecoxib producing coronary thrombosis and heart attack emerged. This created a considerable dilemma as to whether or not to abandon the study. As it happened, we were using Celecoxib, and in much smaller doses, and only for a week or so. As you can see, a study might unravel despite the best planning. It took another nine years!

I was introduced to the nomenclature of the CONSORT guidelines, such as numbers of patients needed to treat and statistical proof. After nine years we had shown no advantage in terms of primary outcomes (e.g. tolerance of oral fluids), but there appeared to be a considerable reduction in paralytic ileus, and no serious cardiac or renal side effects. We submitted our results via research papers to no less than three prestigious journals, all of which rejected the manuscript. Finally, Simon Brookes asked his overseas colleagues for an independent (ie nonsurgical) view, and the work was accepted into *Alimentary Pharmacology and Therapeutics*. We were very ably assisted by **Kristin McLaughlin**, who was then a medical student but had been with the General Practice Department. Kristin was forensic in her approach.

We had an interesting indication that paralytic ileus was much reduced in the COX 2 treated group. To mount another RCT was not practicable in terms of numbers, so I embarked on a clinical study of my own treated patients. Emerging during this time clinical concerns were raised that COX inhibitors reduced anastomotic healing, and that it increased dehiscence, which is a devastating problem. **Dr Devinder Raju** was our senior registrar, and he analysed the data. The paralytic ileus rate in the treated group was 7% as compared to the going rate of 15%. This was not the promise of the initial study, but a significant improvement nonetheless. Moreover, the leak rate was 0.7% - as defined by radiology (there were no re-operations) – which was well below the going rate of 5%. This was a gratifying result that showed it was safe.

This process amounted to a number of years' work, requiring clinical input, science input, being busy and treating lots of patients, and the help of many people. It required longevity of appointment.

Another example of translation occurred with the arrival of Dr Dinning. In concert with **Nick Spencer and Phil Dinning**, we established detailed manometry of bowel specimens. To accommodate these specimens, Nick had a giant organ bath built, the design of which was a tribute to the Biomedical Engineering Department. As part of that we studied the excised colon in cases of severe constipation, both in the patient the day before surgery, and in the organ bath the day after. We confirmed Dr Spencer's original observations that the motility pattern was restored to normal in the organ bath. There was considerable conjecture as to why, which illustrates the founding principal of having the labs close to the operating theatres, and most of all having interested persons.

A giant organ bath and an entire human colon - recording of activity in severe slow transit constipation.

The preceeding work focusses on the activity of the bowel muscle. **Dr Damien Keating** had a focus on function of the mucosa and the endocrine cells in that layer. He benefitted from the liaison with surgery and was able to study human specimens thus leading to seminal publications.

An entirely different area was that of patients presenting with rectal cancer. This was difficult surgery, often necessitating a permanent or temporary stoma and there were the long-term problems of bowel dysfunction and impotence. Radio/chemotherapy became standard preop treatment in my time, and occasionally (in 20% or so of cases) the tumour would melt away. This raised the possibility of not doing surgery at all, and observing the patient. The first case in which I did this was a young man whom I was lining up for completion surgery. When I described the process and potential complications, he was aghast. A second opinion, some years, and two children later, he still has his rectum.

This started a whole field of clinical endeavour, now crystallised into a clinical trial the RENO (rectal cancer no surgery) study. It had been proposed in South America by Dr Habr-Gama. We were leaders in Australia, and I even gave a keynote address on the subject at the RACS. It takes some courage to not operate on the patient, but there were no increased adverse outcomes.

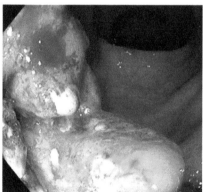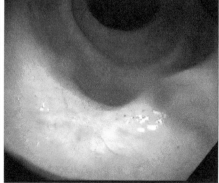

Colonoscopic view of a rectal cancer that disappears with chemoradiotherapy.

Lesson:

We were developing the philosophy of research and clinical medicine fully.

The lab members marking Marcello Costa's retirement in 2022.

Back: *Lukas Wiklendt, Phil Dinning, Adam Humenick.*

Front: *Nan Chen, Marcello Costa, David Wattchow, Simon Brookes, Rochelle Peterson.*

Chapter 12

Overseas Travel

Several trips to Europe and North America, and talking about our work, illustrated the value of what we undertook at Flinders. These were sabbaticals, a form of university leave that acknowledges the value of study elsewhere. They were supported by funding from the RACS and the Clinicians' Special Purpose Fund (CSPF).

On one of these early sabbaticals, I visited the Massachusetts General Hospital in Boston. It was the early 1980s and security was minimal. I was wandering around this famous hospital and entered a rather darkened room. I became aware that I was in the Ether Dome, the very place where the first recorded anaesthetic was administered to a human being. The anaesthetic was given by a dentist, WT Morton. There is a famous painting of this event. The surgery was removal of a carotid body tumour, which is a testing operation. Ether anaesthesia was one year ahead of chloroform (in the UK) as an agent, although it is still a topic of debate as to which was first.

In Boston, I stayed with **Dr Jeff Rich**, a former FMC registrar. He said, "The cost will be two bottles of Grange". I did as he bid, bought two bottles of Grange and carted them in my suitcase, across the USA!

The academic centres and people I visited seemed to really appreciate the combined lab work we were doing. The doyen for bowel work and research was St Mark's Hospital in London. Other people and institutions I found to be significant were Dr Bill Heald, Basingstoke, UK; Dr Roberto De Giorgio, University of Bologna; Professor Gershon, Columbia, New York, the Mayo Clinic and the Cleveland Clinic, USA.

I gave lectures at these august institutions. Several funny incidents resulted. I was waiting on the Tube in London to go to St Marks when signs started flashing, saying, "Expect severe delays". This caused me some panic, as I was not to know that severe delays are matters of minutes in the UK.

St Mark's has a reputation for new ideas and innovation in bowel surgery. It was there I learned of the application of ultrasound to examine the anatomy of the anal sphincter. The surgeons had vast experience. One such surgeon was **Robin Phillips**. Being a visitor and giving a lecture seemed to give me some extra special attention, so I was able to observe him operate. I was craning over his shoulder, and perhaps it crossed his mind that I might fall into the wound. He said, "David, put your hand on my shoulder." He was rather solidly built and was like putting your hand on a rock. Watching him do a standard operation on removing a big set of haemorrhoids, as well as more complex surgeries, was very instructional. I saw the first use of anal ultrasound to obtain accurate images of the internal and external anal sphincters at St Mark's Hospital. Without a doubt, so many insights into anorectal disorders and surgery have come from that ancient hospital. The building was falling down, there is a new one now, but it was the people who were important.

I arranged a visit with **Dr Bill Heald** at Basingstoke, UK, who was the champion of dissection of the mesorectum for rectal cancer. After an interesting day of operating, it came time to catch the train back to London, where I was staying. Bill Heald said he was going to London too, and we should travel together; but not before belting off to his home to pick up a bottle of wine. He went at high speed along the English laneways and pulled over the bridge just as the Intercity train pulled underneath. "David, stop that train!" was the command. So, I sprinted over and placed one foot in the train, the other on the platform, while Dr Heald sauntered over. He didn't have a ticket - "That'll be alright Guv..." With that, he uncorked the bottle.

At another opportunity, I was to give a talk at the university in Bologna, said to be the oldest university in Europe, although others such as Lund in Sweden also claim this honour. My host, **Dr Roberto De Giorgio**, turned up at our hotel, which was rather ostentatious for an impecunious staff surgeon. He arrived on a motorbike with a spare helmet. I donned the helmet, scrambled on the back of the bike and as we wove off into the Italian traffic, my life flashed before my eyes.

On a prior visit to Italy, we had gone to **Dr Carlo Maggi**'s lab in Florence. Marcello Costa was there and we had a most hospitable evening on a Florentine balcony. Those Italians know how to live.

I was unfamiliar with these cities, and especially concerned about the reported violence in New York. Hence, when I was catching the underground to visit Prof Michael Gershon at Columbia University, I tried to be as incognito as possible.

Another time that we were delightfully unaware of risk was when we arrived in Cleveland to visit **Dr Victor Fazio** and his unit. As we had arrived early Margaret and I, with our daughters, wandered down to the Cleveland Park and the museum. The next day in conversation, Dr Fazio said, "You didn't actually walk down there without being mugged?" Thankfully, we survived. I learned an enormous amount on that trip; I saw for the first time the use of lighted retractors and I was later able to buy these for FMC. That is the benefit of travelling - the sharing of ideas and innovations.

Other places and persons I have visited include:

Prof Martin Eastwood at Bart's (St Bartholomew's) Hospital, London

Prof Gordon Lees at Marischal College, Edinburgh

Cleveland Clinic in both southern USA and Ohio, USA, Drs Kelly, Fazio and others

Boston General Hospital

Prof Michael Gershon, New York

Trauma Centre, Sunnybrook Hospital, Toronto

Dr Alison Buchan, Vancouver.

In many cases these were expat Aussies.

Digestive Disease Week (DDW) in the USA was so big it was held in an aircraft hangar, the Moscone Centre in San Francisco. The abstracts were a book. I flew over with **Guy Maddern** (who became Professor of Surgery at Adelaide University) and roomed with **Dr Dick Heddle** in San Francisco. It all seemed very strange and 'New World', as Dvorak's symphony depicts.

I was attending a meeting in Manchester in the UK, and asked a question of the presenter. Across the hallway piped up an old colleague from my days in Bath, Dr Tony Holbrook. With an obvious reference to my clear Australian accent, the Chair, in impeccable English of course, said, "Would my good Antipodean colleague continue his conversation outside?"

It was certainly very educational travelling to these various centres. It was hard work travelling with a young family, and I was always glad to get back home. Nevertheless, the lessons proved invaluable, particularly those gained from visits to surgical centres.

By the way, you cannot buy Weetbix for your young children in North America, it is only possible once you go over the border into Canada. And, you can indeed get decent food in the USA, in New York! Although Margaret and I wondered how things would go when we were taking our youngsters on such long flights and into such unfamiliar cities, things worked out fine. I like to think that these early experiences of world travel instilled in Naomi and Kimberley an appreciation for other countries and a sense of curiosity and adventure.

Lesson:

Travel broadens the mind. Bring ideas back to Australia.

In the UK: College of Surgeons, St Mark's Hospital. In Bologna, the oldest university in Europe. In Friborg, Germany, modern-day noticeboard

Chapter 13

Anorectal Investigations

At Flinders, I inherited the running of our anorectal investigation lab from **Professor Jim Toouli**. Fortuitously, a wonderful senior technician, **Ann Schloithe**, was there, as well as **Dr Gino Saccone**, a hospital scientist who provided continuity.

The control and structure of the anorectum is a rather unique area in the body where there is a smooth muscle (the end of the gut, the internal anal sphincter) surrounded by a skeletal muscle (the external anal sphincter), and it is supplied by both intrinsic and extrinsic nerves (pudendal nerves).

Water perfused manometric systems were being used, and as the patient is conscious, one can assess the conscious squeeze of the external sphincter. Our senior registrar **Dr John McCall** was instrumental in adapting a technique of assessing the conduction velocity in the pudendal nerves. This is where the value of a hospital scientist came in, Dr Saccone manufactured a nerve stimulator and recorder.

We mounted the electrode/recording assembly on a glove, inserted that into the anal canal, and depolarised the pudendal nerves with an electrical pulse, measuring the delay from the pulse to recording the depolarisation of the external sphincter (pudendal nerve terminal motor latency).

We managed to purchase an ultrasound probe, so we now had a comprehensive service where all these techniques were done in the one setting, which is not often the case, worldwide. We were challenged as we had to keep on finding new 'homes', from clinics to a private facility, and finally our own laboratory.

Other developments were critical. Another New Zealander, and a contemporary of Dr McCall, was **Dr John Jarvis**, who established the first database of all this clinical and scientific data. It took years to accumulate a database big enough to commence providing answers to valid questions, but you have to start somewhere. One of our Fellows from the UK, **Dr Arun Loganathan**, used this database to good effect for exploring the conduction of the pudendal nerve, contributions to anal sphincter pressures, and damage by radiotherapy for prostate cancer.

Dr Phillip Dinning joined the staff, replacing Dr Saccone in one of the rare hospital scientist positions. These employment opportunities have been gradually reduced over time in the name of cost saving, and much has been lost in terms of knowledge. Dr Dinning was attracted to working with Profs Brookes and Costa (and then Spencer). We had run out of money, but Gino Saccone was retiring and I championed his employment in that position. It was confirmed by our Divisional Director, **Rob Padbury**. This permanent appointment came to pass and Phil has certainly taken the area forward with the use of solid-state manometry, and now, assessment of the motility of the distal colon.

Dr Rosli, and now **Dr Heitmann**, have both been involved with Dr Dinning in these assessments. They commenced work as junior doctors and gained training positions in surgery. Enrolling for a PhD facilitated those appointments.

To ensure continuity, succession planning and handing on of roles are necessary. At the time of writing this memoir, a young surgeon who has joined the team has largely taken on my role in the clinic. She is **Dr Philippa Rabbitt**, who has also done training in 3D ultrasound, and we have bought such a probe. She brings considerable expertise.

Inevitably, the equipment needed to undertake these studies has required updating, but since that involves considerable cost it has not been easy to do. Fortunately, I generated considerable funds from private practice for the Hospital Equipment Fund, and was able to successfully apply to use that money for equipment, from the initial ultrasound probe right through to the 3D ultrasound and solid-state manometry.

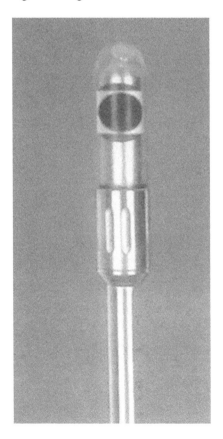

Anorectal probe

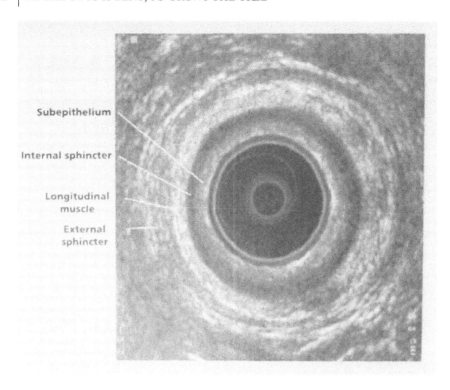

Subepithelium

Internal sphincter

Longitudinal muscle

External sphincter

Ultrasound view of the anal sphincter mechanism

Lesson:

Continue to study and advance clinical medicine.

Chapter 14

Academic Advancement

Over the years I had progressed from Lecturer to Senior Lecturer, to Associate Professor and eventually Professor. In terms of my clinical career this status meant little, but it was important for the Department of Surgery and of Physiology, and for the University.

The University seemed rather remote from the real world of patients, and yet it relied heavily on clinical staff to teach its courses, particularly during the years of practical learning. For this, many of the medical personnel gave their time and expertise freely as that is how they had been taught (i.e. gratis).

After an appropriate length of time, and with a proven record of teaching and research under my belt, it seemed reasonable to apply for advancement to Professor. It is possible to be appointed to this level, but that seems largely for entrepreneurs. Attaining Level E (Professor) at the University is close to impossible for a clinician, although I do know some who have achieved it, one being **Professor Andrew Bersten**. Recognising this, the Academic Senate created a Level D+, and this includes the title of Professor.

The application process is taxing. In this regard, I was greatly aided by the Dean of the day, **Professor Lindon Wing**. My draft came back covered in red ink as Prof Wing had a great eye for detail, which I already knew from clinical interactions. It helped produce a strong application. I'm sure the support of Professor O'Brien, who was by then Head of Surgery at Monash University, helped too.

Professor Villis Marshall had a good saying about academic advancement: "It helps if you have been to Stockholm [for the Nobel Prize] – twice!"

I had trouble encouraging my junior staff not to address me as, "Prof". It is an academic title, after all, and there are some very fine clinicians who don't have academic status. The old joke was, "Don't be cut by the Professor", but I don't think that applies anymore.

At the end of my clinical career, I applied for, and was granted, Emeritus Professor status.

Lesson:

Look at the structure and engine of the university.

Chapter 15

Division of Surgery

From 1990 I worked as a surgeon in the Division of Surgery. **Rob Padbury** became Head of the Division and **David Watson** took on the position of Professor of Surgery. Rob championed quality improvement programs, and David's primary interest was oesophageal diseases and malignancy. This splitting of the roles of what was once the preserve of 'the professor' has been valuable.

It is important to be part of the Division of Surgery. I did the course run by Dr Padbury at the time, to gain insight into the methods of clinical improvement. This was a foreign language to me, and my eyes were opened by the new approach. An interest in quality cuts across medicine, nursing, physiotherapy, and so on. It includes anyone with a prime interest in patient outcome and betterment. In the Division, it revolved around the establishment of best practice, forming a protocol of that practice, communicating and enacting it, and evaluating the intervention.

An enterprise such as this requires personnel to make it work. In our case, some of the people involved were **Margaret Martin**, **Margaret Walker**, **Kerry Leaver** and **Bev Thomas**. They did the hard work of cajoling the consultants, nurses and others, and writing and promulgating the protocols. The protocols were synthesised over several iterations, and their impact was studied. The cycle was to plan – do – study – act. This was to become a mantra for practice improvement in the Division. Results were measured in various ways, but ultimately it was pleasing to see a gradual reduction in mortality across the Division.

Bev Thomas and Margaret Walker

Using a Clinical Practice Improvement

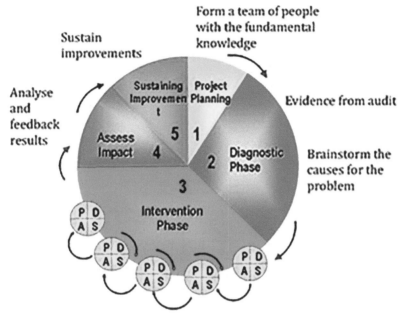

Identify the problem

Form a team of people
with the fundamental
knowledge

Sustain
improvements

Analyse
and
feedback
results

Evidence from audit

Brainstorm the
causes for the
problem

Plan and test interventions

I initiated several of the protocols. The first was for the management of patients presenting with haemorrhage from the lower gut, as I perceived great variation in their treatment and was keen for a more standardised approach. The second was a rationalisation of prophylaxis for venous thromboembolism, which is a big problem in major case surgery.

I needed to form a team, and a member of that team for the VTE project was **Professor Gallus**, who was a world expert on the subject of VTE. The measurement of outcomes and adherence to the protocol were important. A long-term view is needed in order to achieve advances. We all think we have contemporary knowledge of what is best in medicine, but that may not be so.

An important feature of the Division of Surgery is the high number of surgeons with a PhD, and they are good surgeons! Attaining this degree is a hallmark of commitment and talent, and some have continued to contribute to research throughout their working lives.

I was Clinical Head of Gastrointestinal Surgery for 17 years. This involved regular meetings with all the surgeons, and they proved to be a most harmonious group. My job was to set an agenda and summarise the views of the group, as well as constructing a lecture programme. It was enlightening to have other hospital staff share their insights and experience in many of these lectures.

A somewhat unique feature of the Division is that we held an annual Convocation. This was at the instigation of Dr Padbury, our Director. The focus was on quality improvement projects, and it was therefore of wide interest to nurses, doctors and even administrators. It is held off-site and apart from anything else, it is a day of camaraderie. The meeting concludes with a dinner and an occasional address by a guest speaker, often a retiring staff member. Many eloquent, insightful and thought-provoking presentations have been given at the annual Convocations.

I have presented at the Convocation on a number of occasions chiefly about our research and quality projects like improving the time from diagnosis to appendicectomy.

Eventually, it happened that I came to give a 'retirement' address. I tried something a little different by presenting a slide show, set to music, of my various travels in Australia. Many of the surgeons I had helped to train attended, and I was rather humbled to have a spontaneous standing ovation at the end of the presentation.

There was a dent in the wall of the old emergency theatre. The story goes that it was put there by a vascular surgeon who was a big rugby-playing chap. He was doing an emergency aneurysm late one night, and he could not get the graft material he wanted. It is told that the anaesthetist, who was dozing, woke up to see the surgeon head butting the wall.

In my time as a surgeon, I witnessed the construction of new operating theatres at Flinders, and they have increased from six to ten. This came about at the recommendation of **John Menadue**, who wrote a report detailing the need in Southern Adelaide. This is where governments can do useful major capital works. While it was somewhat painful to be working in the theatres with a jackhammer going next door, we now have a really good theatre complex. It enabled a reorganisation of emergency services, to deal with the ever-escalating emergency load. On the ground the project was very capably overseen by Chief Operating Room **Nurse Lea West**, and Administrative Officer **Frank Zotti**. I believe these theatres should be called 'The Lea West Operating Theatres'. Frank Zotti epitomised what a good administrator can do.

In the early hours of one morning, I was operating on a patient with a bleeding ulcer. The patient had lost a lot of blood and I called my registrar to come in quickly and assist. The next day he looked a little wan.

"What's the matter?"

"Dr Wattchow, I got a speeding ticket coming in last night."

"How fast were you going?"

He didn't answer but he must have been moving at a fair clip because the fine was $900. Moreover, it was his mother's car, the fine was waived in the end.

When getting stuck into a big case that might take three to four hours, you need some fat and calories in the system. It is probably as important as any technical know-how. I was fond of saying to the registrars, "This is a bacon and eggs case." Muesli and coffee would not suffice, and will be well and truly gone after an hour or two. Bacon and eggs will last all day.

I would caution the registrars about making hasty decisions. Human beings are the most impatient of creatures, often wanting instant solutions and cures. Mostly it takes time and reflection to come to the best decision.

One piece of advice I offer my registrars is that there is a way of preventing anastomotic leaks, "Don't do any anastomoses." Equally, one can prevent post-op complications and deaths by not doing any surgery.

More good advice to the registrars, "The main purpose of the heart is to supply blood to the bowel." There is an element of truth in this, as a poor cardiac output spells bad news for bowel surgery. And, "You don't have to be that smart to be a doctor – but you do need to be careful."

Here is some great advice from an accomplished vascular surgeon, **Dr Bob Foreman**, "The best (aortic) aneurysm is a boring aortic aneurysm!" Certainly, if you get a ruptured aortic aneurysm in the theatre, gaining control of the aorta can get your pulse rate up!

When there is major bleeding, whatever you do, don't panic. Stick a finger on the vessel, take a deep breath and then sort it out. Bleeding from a big vein is far harder to deal with than bleeding from an artery. I have joked about the 'vein of pain', in reference to the right colic vein buried amongst fat. If it is pulled off in a right hemicolectomy, considerable haemorrhage occurs as it is not far to the portal vein (a big vessel), more exposure, pressure and careful dissection are needed before gaining control. It is a mistake to 'smash and grab'.

An academic turned up with peritonitis. My preop advice was quick, "We need to look inside, and you might end up with a bag." It happened, although ultimately the stoma was reversed. I explained later the reasons for my brevity. "Oh, don't apologise," was the reply "You did what you had to do."

The Fellowship exam is rather testing and seen as a major hurdle to registrars, and I made it a habit to call them when they were successful (or not). On one occasion, I called the registrar **Dr Nigel DaSilva** and asked about the exam. "Oh that," he replied. "It was easy compared to a colorectal ward round."

Multidisciplinary Teams (MDTs) had input from surgeons, radiologists pathologists, and so on. On one occasion we were discussing a case where the patient had right colon cancer and gallstones. I mentioned that we would remove the gallbladder at the time of the colectomy. A junior RMO piped up, "You can't do that - you are not a biliary surgeon!" I reassured the team that I had removed many gallbladders and regardless, help was not far away.

Audit has become an important activity at Flinders, with accurate data collection via the CART tool devised by an orthopaedic surgeon,

Peter Tamblyn. We have an annual audit and interstate reviewer of each unit's activity. Each death is thoroughly audited, including a statewide audit and independent assessment under qualified privilege – South Australian Audit of Surgical Mortality (SAASM).

Lesson:

It is valuable to have close colleagues.

Chapter 16

Colleagues

I cannot emphasise enough the value of working with good colleagues. The Division of Surgery was created by Jim Watts to be collegial, and it has remained that way under the guidance of Professor Marshall, then Professor Padbury.

You need to be able to rely on the help of colleagues throughout medicine. I have one important piece of advice, get on the phone and ring them up. Using bits of paper and circuitous referrals doesn't work that well. Nothing beats the value and immediacy of conversation.

Everyone brings their own expertise:

Rob Padbury: Head of the Division and champion of quality improvement. Rob helped establish liver transplantation in South Australia. He did a PhD in innervation of the gallbladder and bile ducts. He is a liver surgery expert and has published in this area. Examiner for the RACS.

Neil McIntosh: The first Chief Resident in Surgery at Flinders. Neil is a consummate surgeon who spent many years working with top surgeons in the UK, while bringing up a young family. He developed a very busy private practice based in the Blackwood area, but always had time for the FMC and its patients. One example was a case of a ruptured spleen being managed too conservatively. The boy was seriously ill and dying. Neil was on call and he came in, removed the damaged spleen, and thus saved the patient's life. Apart from anything else, Neil was basically a kind man and is fondly remembered by his patients and staff.

Jim Sweeney: A consummate colorectal surgeon and firm, but fair, man. Jim had trained at St Mark's. He once advised me to have confidence in the junior staff and not micromanage them, and it proved to be good counsel. He gave a good opinion on tough cases. Chief Examiner for the RACS, Chair of the Colorectal Surgical Society of Australia and New Zealand (CSSANZ).

Richard Sarre: Richard spent several years in the Cleveland Clinic. He was well worth shadowing to learn bowel surgery. He had some great jokes. Once, on a ward round, he said, "You only have a limited number of steps in life, then you're done." This was to make the point not to go to and fro, all over the hospital.

Paul Hollington: Head of the Colorectal Unit. Paul did a PhD in molecular genetics of bowel cancer (homeotic genes), for which I was the Clinical Supervisor. Examiner for the RACS.

Tom Wilson: Senior Hepatobiliary Surgeon and general contributor to the Division. Chief Examiner for the RACS.

David Watson: Current Chair of Surgery. He has done a number of randomised trials in laparoscopic surgery and has a good lab investigating oesophageal cancer. Matthew Flinders Distinguished Professor.

John Chen: Liver Transplant Surgeon. John is a very hard worker. He did a PhD in pancreatitis, and ran a database of pancreatic surgery.

David Hill: A Senior Surgeon at FMC; mentor then colleague. David provided excellent back-up for me when I went away. He was dedicated to teaching. A lesson for me was never to criticise one's colleagues for management while you were away, they might not be available next time!

Recent Appointments:

Dayan DeFontgalland: My previous PhD student.
Philippa Rabbitt: Interested in pelvic floor problems.
Luigi Sposato: Resettled from Melbourne; did a study of our early experience in the non-operative management of rectal cancer.
Mark Brooke-Smith: PhD, liver surgeon.
Susan Gan: Hepatobiliary surgeon.

We have been joined by surgeons from Noarlunga, the Repat and Modbury:

Dr Worley (RACS President, SA),
Dr Yeow
Dr Schoemaker
Dr Whalan.

There is a theme of completing PhDs and appointments in surgery. Equally, there is the practice of contributing in other areas, such as acting as RACS Examiners (these are huge tasks) and teaching. It is important to contribute something above and beyond one's clinical appointment and it is just as important to be a good clinician who has credibility.

In recent times some notable surgeons have retired. Jim Watts passed away and his funeral gathering at Fox Creek Winery, which he established, was a gathering of Flinders' past.

Richard Willing should not be forgotten, he was a senior gastroenterologist who worked closely with Jim Watts. Richard had wide interests in farming and exploration of the Flinders Ranges. He would take us on 'medical' ward rounds, and on one occasion had a long conversation with an alcoholic patient. We didn't know the patient was confabulating due to Korsakoff's psychosis (Vit B6 deficiency), and wondered how this senior physician knew this character.

I have had varying jobs in administrative roles, including Head of Colorectal Surgery, Surgical Supervisor, Head of Gastrointestinal Surgery. Generally, I found five years was about the right length of time for these positions. It was always best to take advice from colleagues, and rare to have to make an executive decision. I have run a surgical lectures series, often bringing in outside experts to talk to the assembled consultants and students. An instructive talk was by **Dr Steve Graves**, an orthopaedic surgeon, about the establishment of a prosthetic joint registry. The hallmarks were simplicity and universality, and by these means the problems with cadmium in hip prostheses were identified.

A memorable incident involved a man who collapsed on a plane flight from Sydney to Adelaide. Dr Hill and I were returning from a conference. A call went out, "Is there a doctor on board?" Getting a well-built man over the seat rail and into the back of the plane is not easy, I can tell you. The hostesses came up with an IV cannula. It took multiple attempts to get it in, a pharmacopeia of drugs appeared, and a defibrillator, that fortunately was not needed. There was only half a litre of IV fluid and Dr Hill was a good drip stand. The man revived somewhat and the Captain called through, "I can divert to Canberra." To which I replied, "That is not necessary, head straight to Adelaide!" Otherwise, we would have been considerably delayed. The patient was wriggling around by then and I had to get him into a seat for landing. After we landed, the paramedics arrived and took over and the passengers were as quiet as church mice. That broke the boredom!

A well-remembered case was the 'exploding colon'. I was doing an emergency total colectomy for a dilated, toxic colon. I removed it intact and passed the specimen to my assistant, "Have you got it?" "Yes, sir". Whereupon his grip loosened and the full colon landed on the floor and burst. Shit went everywhere except, thankfully, in the open abdomen!

I would joke with the Registrars that if you wanted to be good at surgery you had to practise a lot. I 'betcha' that's why Roger Federer is so good at tennis. Concert pianists are the same and I think the famous golfer Arnold Palmer said, "The more I practise, the luckier I get!"

We had many airline analogies such as checklists. A favourite concerned learning and experience where you would not fly on a plane if the pilot was thumbing through the 'How to Fly Manual'. One would hope they had done it before, many times, and with someone experienced.

I joked often, "There is only one way of avoiding complications - don't operate." I've cut everything in the abdomen except the bile duct. Well, not cut it inadvertently. The main thing is to recognise difficulties when they happen and to fix them.

I did learn an embarrassing lesson about commenting on a registrar's weight. I thought she was about to give birth and I expressed concern as to how the pregnancy was going. "I've had the baby, Dr Wattchow," she replied. Whoops! To this day she laughs at that incident.

One day I was seeing a patient on the gynaecology ward (not my home ward). A nurse came up to me requesting drip orders be written. She thought I was the intern! Now, I did retain some youthful looks, in fact in a photo taken in Third Year Medicine, I still looked like I was just out of primary school. She twigged I was not the intern, the RMO perhaps, or the registrar. "You're not the boss?" she questioned. "I'm afraid so, but I can still do the fluid orders for you."

There were broader issues too. The Colorectal Surgical Society of Australia and New Zealand (CSSANZ) formed at this time and I joined this group. I contributed to assessing research proposals, and received a thank you call from the President, **Ian Jones**. The Society was most generous in supporting research students. I was awarded *Life Membership* on retirement, a most humbling experience.

Underpinning it all was excellent secretarial support. **Stenia Smith** followed by **Beryl Sutton** were secretaries on the unit. Beryl was, and is, a mad keen Port Adelaide supporter, and this was the source of some great repartee. The saying, "When you want a job done, ask a busy person", typified Beryl. She would tell me that my request was at the end of the queue, but invariably it was done by the end of the day. Often, outpatient letters dictated in the morning were done by close of day. Other staff who come to mind were **Rosemary Wilde** (Secretary to Prof Watts), **Pauline Archer**, and **Michelle Raymond**.

The Gastrointestinal Surgical Group in 2012: Piers Gatenby (SR UK), Paul Hollington, Justin Bessell, Lilian Kow, Susan Gan, Mayank Bandari (SR), David Watson, Andrew Chew, John Chen, Mark Brooke-Smith, Richard Sarre, Tom Wilson, David Hill, David Wattchow, Jim Sweeney, Tim Bright.

The Colorectal Unit in 2006: David Wattchow, Paul Hollington, Jim Sweeney, Richard Sarre, David Hill.

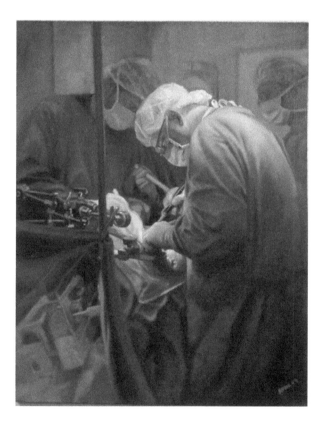

Painting of Rob Padbury operating; in the Department of Surgery.

Lessons:

Work with good colleagues and get along with them all, wherever possible. They are talented folk with legitimate points of view.

Do not be hasty to judge character. People mature with time. Many have had good careers in medicine despite a seemingly slow start.

Chapter 17

Medical Students

I have observed considerable changes in the teaching and selection of students over time. The days of almost individualised teaching that we experienced as students have largely disappeared. Classes have increased in size and student selection has changed, to include a rigorous process of examinations (GAMSAT) and interview. As a 17-year-old, I simply would not have made today's selection! Medicine became a postgraduate course at Flinders, as did most Medicine courses in Australia. The process is so rigorous that only the brightest candidates with proven commitment are selected. I think that is a primary reason for success.

As students, we attended autopsies. They are rare these days. We even performed some of them. On one occasion, I was left performing such an examination on a complex case that had puzzled the medical team involved. They turned up, wanting some answers, and were not impressed that a student was doing the autopsy!

The curriculum has become much more proscribed. Problem-based learning (PBL) became a popular concept. I wrote one such case on rectal cancer and it was used for many years. There was tremendous goodwill from the clinical staff for teaching. Eventually the PBL tutors were professional teachers, as the demands of clinical medicine escalated.

Teaching became much more regimented. A good example of this was the Structured Clinical Instruction Module (SCIM), whereby we taught a whole class, in small groups, about examination of hernias and the acute abdomen. Therefore, all students were exposed to a core of problems but it is easy to be lost in a crowd, and few appeared to prepare for these sessions. It remained that Senior Surgeons would set aside their time for these sessions, and that is a huge resource donated to the University. I used to quiz the students on inguinal anatomy until one bright spark manoeuvred the dicussion to heart attacks – to avoid the questioning!

An education section that evolved was led by **Dr David Prideaux**. Various educators would visit, and I was particularly struck by a speaker on the topic 'Assessment drives education'. This was another way of saying the students will study the relevant material to pass the exams.

The importance of education was emphasised from the outset with the appointment of an 'Educator', **Dr Russell Linke**.

We all contributed to the marking, if not the setting, of the Ordered Structured Clinical Examinations (OSCEs). These were conducted at the end of Third Year, out of four years. They were somewhat akin to our own examinations at the end of 5th year, to allow a final year unencumbered by examinations. This involved clinical exams that would be held on a Saturday morning, and written papers. The questions were fairly basic, as they ought to be as it required a grasp of clinical medicine to pass. It was, and is, a enormous test, and the students were very nervous.

At the end of the day you judge the finished product, and somewhere along the way the students turned into doctors and were invariably good interns and RMOs. Indeed, that is one of the themes of Samuel Shem's *The House of God*, based on the Beth Israel hospital in Boston, in which a naïve junior is thrashed into becoming a good doctor by the end of his internship, and, somewhat of a cynic. Shem (a pseudonym) published this in 1978 and became a psychiatrist.

As an aside, I have observed that it seems much harder to become selected for advanced training. I almost certainly benefited from experiencing different areas of medicine, such as general medicine and neurosurgery, before settling on general surgery. Much of our final selection was guided, or influenced, by mentors. Now, it seems that young doctors make up their minds early, work towards the chosen goal, and accept that it may take some years. This is most marked in surgery, and orthopaedics, plastics and general surgery especially come to mind.

An example of the change in teaching is in anatomy. Understanding human anatomy is basic to the practice of medicine, and this has been enunciated since the beautiful woodcuts of the Belgian anatomist Andreas Vesalius. There were only a few books and atlases in my day, but the resources are now vast. While it is possible to dissect the human body electronically, there is nothing like the real thing.

Later in my career, when I joined the Clinical Advisory Group to lend some perspective on student teaching, the new language of medical education was most foreign to me.

Lesson:

We were all students once!

Chapter 18

Registrars

I have had the good fortune of working with many talented registrars. These doctors occupy a senior role in the hospital (and indeed in society), and they shoulder much of the emergency load. They are often preparing for the final Fellowship exam in Surgery. This exam is focused on common-sense and safety, and I have helped many to prepare for it. I have helped with the courses run by General Surgeons Australia to this end.

Registrars are human beings too, with families and lives outside medicine, although we can forget that they as they are fairly senior in the medical hierarchy. I left two registrars to do an intestinal anastomosis, and they shared it. That is, each did half of the procedure. It leaked, which led to the quip from the junior, "Never do things by halves."

A feature of a place the size of Flinders is that it attracts Senior Registrars. These people have all attained their FRACS and are embarking on a specialist career in an aspect of surgery. That has become formalised in later years, so that we now have trainees in Colorectal Surgery. Our Unit (and the whole of the Surgery Division) reserves places for trainees from overseas. They bring a lot to the unit and work very hard. The people from overseas invariably live by the beach and really enjoy their time in Australia.

Notable fellows have been:
John McCall: From New Zealand.
Rajeev Kapoor: From Ludhiana, India.
John Jarvis: From New Zealand; helped set up a database for anorectal manometry.
Anders Tottrup: From Denmark.
David Vernon: From New Zealand; I gave him a lift home once when his bike was wrecked as it was on top of someone else's car and they exited the car park but there wasn't enough clearance.
Carey Gall: An Aussie, now in Tasmania; our first Colorectal Fellow; he wrote a paper on oesophageal cancer with me as a junior.
Jo Dale: From Brisbane; a talented surgeon
Arun Loganathan: From the UK; did several studies on anorectal physiology.
Philippa Rabbitt: Now a member of the Unit.
Hidde Kroon: From the Netherlands.
Chris Lauder: From England; became an Australian.
George Barreto: From Goa, India.

You could learn a lot from the Fellows. Anders Tottrup told me about Furchgott, who won the Nobel Prize for the discovery of EDRF (later found to be nitric oxide). Indeed, most Nobel Prizes have come from the basic sciences, which was detailed nicely by Rose Ryall, a Senior Scientist in the Department who took over from Prof Marshall as the interim Chair.

It is important to train the next generation of registrars. After all, they could be operating on you some day. This is what was done for us gratis, and we should do the same now.

Lesson:

It is good to work with talented registrars near the end of their training. They will help you out a lot.

Chapter 19

Anaesthetists

One simply cannot do surgery without anaesthesia. Agents of anaesthesia have improved from ether to inhalational (but volatile) agents, and in recent times, the intravenous agent propofol. Next, the one-shot spinal before the commencement of a laparotomy came in. Post-op pain relief vastly improved with the use of PCAs, epidurals and dedicated pain nurses and rounds.

Some characters I have encountered in this field are:

Garry Phillips: A very strong man, gentle too. Second Chair of Anaesthesia. Garry had a strong emphasis on protocols in standardising care, specifically in trauma care.

Michael Cousins: An anaesthetist; first Professor of Anaesthesia.

Peter Lillie: A real 'go to' anaesthetist who appeared to have an intrinsic feel for the patient. Peter was rather free thinking. He was involved in liver transplantation from the outset. At the start of a conversation, he would remark, "What's happening in the big bad world of surgery?"

Gerry Neumeister: A booming South African who instilled confidence in his patients. We did much major surgery together in the private hospital. Gerry introduced one-shot spinals for pain control. He could cut to the chase, for example, when I had a young patient bleeding out after a slipped ligature and she was very ill, he was totally under control with the resuscitation.

Graeme McLeay: A 'quiet Australian' who never seemed to be under pressure. Graeme gave me a nice compliment on his retirement, "I have worked with many surgeons and you are one of the best."

Andrew Hardy: A senior anaesthetist and a funny man.

John Currie: A dour Scot who seemed to love his craft. He paraphrased an old saying, "No good deed shall ever go unpunished", attributed to Oscar Wilde. I was to learn the truth of this sarcasm later.

Mark Markou: A young anaesthetist and protégé of Dr Lillie, with a great command of statistics.

And there were many more.

Anaesthesia has become very safe but things can go wrong, and suddenly. I was about to embark upon a gut fistula case from the Northern Territory, but I never put the knife to skin as the patient arrested as soon as the muscle relaxant (Rocuronium) was given. A serum tryptase was sky high, indicating an allergic reaction, rare but real. There ensued a difficult conversation with the man's wife.

Lesson:

Valuable colleagues make surgery possible.

Chapter 20

Gynaecology

Prominent Gynaecologists were **Todd Sanders, Simon Hyde** and **Sellva Paramasivam**.

Over time, I assisted my gynaecological colleagues and helped out with many cases of, usually advanced, ovarian and uterine cancer. By and large, these malignancies were much more widespread than bowel cancer and it was important to remove as much cancer as possible (called debulking). This often involved resecting various pieces of bowel, including the rectum. On many occasions a stoma was required. These patients had major surgery and support from the ICU was needed. The patient would have chemotherapy once recovered, and good results could be obtained if the tumour was chemosensitive.

Radiotherapy often formed part of patient management. In the past, large, non-targeted doses were given. Some lives were saved by such treatments, but at the cost of damage to the small intestine by a radiation-induced endarteritis. This would cause small bowel narrowing and obstruction, and extensive resections were required to remedy it. Home

TPN tended to be needed in these cases. When hyperbaric oxygen came along, that helped some cases.

There is a considerable overlap between gynaecology and bowel surgery. I have helped the obstetricians when the anal sphincter was torn at childbirth. I have repaired the sphincter, by dissecting out the anal sphincter and doing an overlapping repair. I had close working relationships with **Drs Elinor Atkinson** and **Jane Wood**, who dealt with many of these problems. All in all, they were challenging cases but some good results were obtained.

Lesson:

Gynaecology is a challenging area that still has major hurdles.

Chapter 21

Ophthalmology

The Department of Ophthalmology seemed like a somewhat remote and separate department, but it was a shining light at Flinders. It had a very strong and direct Head of Department, **Professor Doug Coster**, and a very talented senior Scientist, **Professor Keryn Williams**. Amongst many things, Professor Williams was instrumental in establishing the corneal graft registry.

I did an elective term in ophthalmology as a medical student and a term as a resident. My experience was when operations for cataracts were major exercises. The patients were admitted, surgery took hours, and they were nursed with their heads between sandbags for several days to prevent movement! The procedure has moved along and the surgery is so refined that 10 cases per list are done as day patients, under local anaesthesia.

Professor Coster has detailed the development of the Ophthalmology Department. On one occasion, the famous eye surgeon Fred Hollows was visiting and lecturing and he and Professor Coster obviously had differences of opinion.

A top appointment was Keryn Williams. She was a dedicated and quiet scientist and she encouraged a generation of clinician/scientists. She was awarded the AC for her work. The AC is a Companion of Australia, the highest national honour , one does not need to be a bombastic person to make an impact. I do recall one time when there was a rally of scientists during what was an anti-vaccination campaign. This was well before Covid. Professor Williams was quoted as saying, "You don't hear of polio these days – due to science."

Lesson:

Ophthalmology, a great example of combining medicine and science.

Chapter 22

Gastroenterology

Gastrointestinal surgery is closely allied with gastroenterology. An early contact with gastroenterologists was with **Derwin Williams**, who was a very busy doctor. He taught me how to scope in the days where there were no video screens, only a beam splitter placed on the eyepiece. He must have been enormously patient.

Now examination of the gastrointestinal tract is routine. I came across, and introduced to Flinders, the tattooing of lesions, initially with sterilised Indian ink; and the use of argon beam coagulation in the treatment of lesions, which was initially angiodysplastia in the rectum due to radiation for prostate cancer.

Derwin's protégé, **Dr Sandy Craig**, followed in his vein and became a very busy gastroenterologist. He referred countless patients to me, many with colon cancers, and this helped underpin my research endeavours.

In the early days, **Dr John Dent** was Head of Gastroenterology. He had interests in measuring upper gastrointestinal motility, and devised the 'Dent Sleeve' to enable continuous measurement of pressures in the lower oesophageal sphincter and pylorus. By such means, transient lower oesophageal relaxations and isolated pyloric pressure waves were discovered. Attempts were made to commercialise this device. Dr Dent was the Chair of the Gastroenterology Society in Australia. He successfully diverted drug company funds into scholarships, which was a major achievement.

I became a colleague of **Professor Graeme Young**. He was a champion of research and was involved in the National Bowel Cancer Screening Project. This involved the testing of faeces for occult blood as an indicator of bowel cancer. There was good evidence it was effective in leading to a diagnosis of earlier stage bowel cancer.

He had an excellent scientific team who were at the forefront of identifying circulating tumour DNA as a marker of cancer:

Dr Peter Bampton had considerable interest in gut motility. He had done a PhD with Phil Dinning and Ian Cooke in Sydney. Thus, he accumulated many cases of irritable bowel syndrome, a hard-to-treat condition that is still poorly understood. We shared many cases.

Malcolm McKinnon was integral in setting up the Endoscopy Unit. He was involved in setting up a winery on retirement.

Adrian Chung was a young gastroenterologist who trained with Michael Burke in the eastern states and was an expert in advanced techniques in colonoscopy.

Other skilled gastroenterologists were Darren Mounkley, Alan Wigg, Sam Edwards and Laurie Chitti.

The field improved greatly in my time, for example, the development of PPIs and the discovery of Helicobacter. Immune modulation with monoclonal antibodies developed, over and above steroids, such that surgery for inflammatory bowel disease (in particular proctocolectomy and ileoanal pouch formation) became infrequent.

Their efforts were underpinned by a whole cluster of skilled endoscopy nurses.

Lesson:

There are valuable colleagues in every field.

Chapter 23

ICU and Home TPN

In any major hospital these days, the Intensive Care Unit is important to the conduct of business. These doctors and nurses are skilled in providing support to the sickest patients. I was often involved as my patients would end up in the ICU for management of septicaemia plus, surgery formed part of the definitive management.

At FMC, I worked with many intensivists: **Garry Philips**, **Al Vedig**, **Andrew Bersten**, **Andrew Holt**, **Evan Everest**.

Dr Holt was the expert for home TPN in the state, so complex patients with gut failure would gravitate to FMC. Invariably, he would ask my opinion about the role of surgery. On occasion the problem could be remedied and the patient was able to resume nourishment. One notable case had had multiple surgeries, and had an enterocutaneous fistula, connection of the gut to the skin, from surgery elsewhere. After a long period of home TPN, surgery was undertaken to restore her nourishment and close the fistula. Another patient had complex surgery and tubes in every section of the gut. A detailed review and investigation showed that most of these were causing harm and they were withdrawn, with successful restoration of feeding. On other occasions there were multiple connections of the gut to the skin. The best one could accomplish was to resect most of the gut and create one good stoma, thus making life easier with the patient needing to accept a life of intravenous nutrition.

Andrew Bersten was a Senior ICU Physician who was also a full university Professor. He personified the idea of research underpinning good clinical practice.

Evan Everest was from New Zealand. Apart from his ICU expertise, he contributed at a State level in trauma retrieval and care. If you needed someone coming down the line from a helicopter, he was your man!

These are just some examples of going above and beyond.

Lesson:

Teamwork will give the best results.

Chapter 24

Medical Oncology

I worked closely with the Medical Oncologists and was to observe significant changes in this field. This was not an easy area of medicine, as most patients have advanced malignancies.

Some talented folk I encountered were **Bogda Koczswara, Chris Karapetis, Amitesh Roy** and **Sina Vatandoust**. The first Medical Oncologist was **Trevor Malden**. This was a time when it had been demonstrated that chemotherapy reduced recurrence rate in node-positive bowel cancer.

Lymphoma, and even leukaemias, became treatable by chemo and bone marrow transplantation. A first step for lymphoma was node biopsy, and I would always get these patients into surgery at the earliest opportunity to allay concerns.

Dr Koczswara championed the concept of survivorship of cancer. Generally, only a few had focused on the patients who would survive the cancer and their ongoing care.

I was at a national meeting where a paper was quoted from the famous *New England Journal of Medicine* on the role of kRas and chemotherapy. The lead author was Chris Karapetis, one of 'our' oncologists.

Recalling the study on rectal cancer and the observation of when it melted away with radiotherapy, Dr Sina Vatandoust took the running with this and now there is a nationwide study called the RENO (rectal cancer no surgery) study.

Lesson:

Chemotherapy is part of the whole patient treatment.

Chapter 25

Flinders Private Hospital

Stage 4 of Flinders Medical Centre was never built, but a private hospital sprung up in its place. Integral to its construction were **Byron Gregory**, **Margot Strachan**, then latterly **Angela McCabe**. I transferred many of the lessons from Flinders Medical Centre to Flinders Private Hospital (FPH).

FPH had the good fortune to be just across the corridor. I had not planned to do much work in private practice but ended up doing quite a lot because of the colocation. I was allowed one half session a week, which I coalesced into one operating day per fortnight.

This was often a very full day. The maximum number of surgeries was on a day when I did a coloanal anastomosis for rectal cancer, a low anterior resection for rectal cancer, a high anterior resection, a right hemicolectomy and an extensive small bowel resection for Crohn's disease! It was only made possible for me to achieve this by the excellent team of anaesthetists and nurses and assistants along with the back-up of an ICU.

I had excellent assistants in the Private Hospital, invariably they were doing PhDs. I had one trainee who was permanently agitated. There was a circumstance where he had to dash out. The Theatre Nurse (Cath Butcher) and I just looked at each other and exhaled a sigh. Thank goodness for the quiet! It is best to be calm when operating.

The proximity of the two hospitals meant that on occasion I took a sick patient across to FMC for an emergency operation, as FMC had 24-hour operating theatres. This was a life-saving manoeuvre and would only happen when a theatre was not available in FPH. It was a good example of the colocation of the two facilities.

I did rounds early at FPH. I was legendary for hiding the nursing observation charts so I could complete the reviews. The nurses would cotton on to the hiding places – I even ended up hiding them under the desk. The only time I was somewhat short with the staff was when the fluid balance charts were incomplete, as this is critical information.

From the days the doors opened, I did 20 years of practice in FPH, and ended up cutting the cake at the 20-year celebrations! I feel honoured to have underpinned a lot of work in FPH.

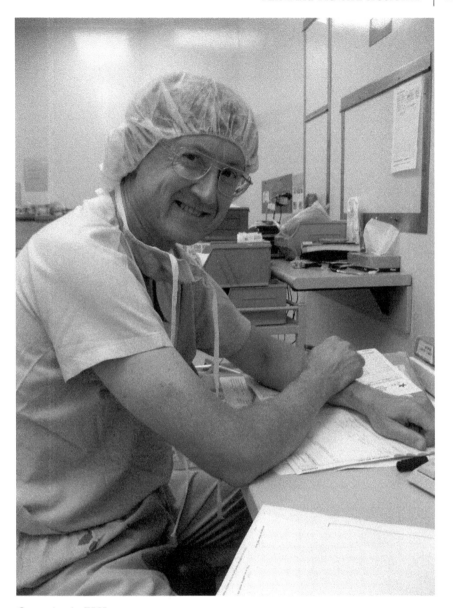

Operating in FPH

A modern view of Flinders Medical Centre, including Flinders Private Hospital, the Cancer Centre and the car park

Lesson:

The end result may be achieved in a number of ways. Make the most of opportunities that are presented to you.

Chapter 26

Deans and CEOs

During my experience at the Medical School, now a College, there have been a number of Deans. The position of Dean is very powerful and they each have placed their own stamp on the job. The position of Chief Executive Officer (CEO) also creates a very important print on the hospital.

The first Dean was the incomparable **Gus Fraenkel**, who set up the physical and intellectual basis of the institution. The Medical Library bears Professor Fraenkel's name in his memory. In the fabulous cartoon of him assembling the school from dominoes, the cartoonist from the Medical Illustration and Media Department even captured his disarming thick spectacles!

Laurie Geffen followed, his contributions were significant. Along came the energetic **John Chalmers**, who seemed capable of just about everything, so running a medical school would have been no sweat for him. Professor Chalmers was so highly regarded that there is an annual lecture named for him. The 'John Chalmers Oration' is given by august lecturers from throughout the country and world.

Next was **Ross Kalucy** and then **Nick Saunders**. The latter I did not know well except that he was a respiratory physician, an entrepreneur and driver of change. The school had gone through much variation and needed a period of consolidation. That was provided by **Professor Lindon Wing**, a physician/pharmacologist with a great eye for detail. He was involved with my application for academic advancement. A clinical case comes to mind that this further illustrates his knowledge. I was consulted on a case of likely phaeochromocytoma (that is, a benign tumour of adrenal gland tissues that releases noradrenaline and thus causes hypertension – albeit a rare cause). Professor Wing was evaluating the case, and noradrenaline levels had been sampled in the bloodstream. These included the superior vena cava, in which the level was high. "That'll be due to drainage via the azygous vein," Lindon deduced, thus demonstrating a vast knowledge of human anatomy, along with physiology. Pleasingly, remembering that imaging was not so good then, a tumour was discovered nestling between the vena cava and the aorta. It was challenging to remove, but I had the benefit of vascular surgeons who were not scared of working close to those vessels.

Lindon moved on and **Paul Worley** took over as Dean. Paul was a GP with a strong focus on rural medicine, and he drove this agenda hard. He expanded the school into campuses at Mt Gambier, Victor Harbor, the Riverland and the Northern Territory. He has moved on to a senior role in coordinating rural health throughout Australia.

Lindon had made a big donation to the University to establish the 'Lindon Wing Scholarship' for research between a combined scientist/clinician team. I helped to evaluate participants in the days before he died. His legacy is perpetuated through the scholarship.

Now we have become a College, **Professor Jonathan Craig** has taken the reins of this rather complex organisation. There is even a new building for Health Sciences. I go there from time to time to give talks to the medical students about careers in medicine; or maybe to a talk on 'translation' of science into medicine at the Centre for Neuroscience.

Flinders Medical Centre Deans: Gus Fraenkel, Laurie Geffen, John Chalmers, Ross Kalucy, Nick Saunders, Lindon Wing, Paul Worley, Jonathan Craig.

Lesson:

A Dean is an influential person who shapes the direction of the school/college.

Chief Executive Officers

The position of Chief Executive Officer at Flinders is most significant, and in my time, I encountered many who held the position.

The first CEO was **John Blandford**. He was from Wales, and he oversaw the construction of FMC. He was followed by **Norman Popplewell**, who was involved in further construction and then John Blandford had another stint. John was a keen photographer, and his pictures adorn the walls of FMC.

Other CEOs have been **Lesley Dwyer**, **Julia Davison**, **Michael Swarcbord**, and recently **Sue O'Neill**. Each has placed their imprint on Flinders Medical Centre.

Gus Fraenkel and Norman Popplewell overseeing the hospital construction.

Gus and John Blandford (first CEO).

Lesson:

A good administrator will lead the institution.

Chapter 27

The Clinicians' Special Purpose Fund

In the early days of the hospital, some far-sighted clinicians set up a philanthropic fund for the effective use of private practice monies, primarily for research and education. The chief proponent was **Dr Michael Sage** from Radiology, then **Dr Bob McRitchie**, a cardiologist. The set-up was quite clever, monies generated were set aside against a person's name and a moiety went to a general pool of funds. The use of the funds was governed by a committee, which applied a strict set of guidelines. I took over from Dr McRitchie, and had a committee of diverse specialists from throughout the hospital for advice.

Traditionally, a lot of money has been passed on to this fund. That is not the case now, as clinicians largely seek to keep all their private practice money.

We have funded a PhD scholarship for clinical trainees for 30 years or more. It has been a great start for many clinicians who could not get funding from traditional sources. In recent times there has been considerable competition for the scholarships, necessitating independent assessments from a number of senior clinicians.

Another substantial contribution was a grant of $1 million towards the construction of the new Cancer Centre. It was **Mr Gary Verstegen**, a member of the admin team at that time, who made this suggestion. That added another floor to this centre.

You have to be careful dealing with other people's money, but it sure is fun giving it away!

There was a stage when we had to fight for these funds. The Government of the day sought to appropriate the money. Thus, commenced two years of meetings with the Department of Health. The solid structure and governance of our own fund was critical at these times. Critical too, was the support of the Australian Medical Association, which proved to be a very powerful force, and the unshakeable resolve of **Bob Bryce**, who was on the CSPF committee at Flinders. There was a State-wide camaraderie in support of these funds.

Government officials are rather imposing, but there was a principle at stake and we persisted. A good outcome was the development of proper governance of the monies, which we already had in place.

The fund generously supports the 'Annual Convocation for Surgery', in recognition of the educational value of the day. It has assisted bringing visitors from overseas, and the Office for Research in recent times.

I was on the committee for 20 years, and was Chairperson for 17 of them. During that period, I revised the operational guidelines and pursued the amalgamation with the Repatriation General Hospital funds. I always felt a main purpose of the fund was an annual PhD scholarship. We would advertise and send applications to august members of the hospital for assessment.

Right at the end, I passed the role of Chairperson onto another member. To my considerable surprise, the committee renamed the 'Clinicians' Special Purpose Fund Committee PhD Scholarship' as the 'David Wattchow PhD Scholarship'!

Lessons:

Partake in activities with a broad interest at heart.

A committee is a democracy, so go with the majority decision.

Use the varying talents of the members.

Awarding the CSPF annual prize to Dr Lito Papanicolas; Dr Aylward, Dr Gordon and Dr Wattchow.

The Clinicians' Special Purpose Fund Committee:

Top (L-R): A/Prof Peter Marshall, Dr Jacob Chisholm, Dr Santosh Poonoose, Prof Bob Bryce

Bottom (L-R): Dr Jeff Bowden, Prof David Wattchow, Ms Dianne Holmes, Dr Evan Everest

Chapter 28

Patients

In all this time, my primary role was that of a clinician at the Flinders Medical Centre. I use the word 'clinician' to encompass much more than technical surgery as it involves a knowledge of medicine and psychology. My full-time appointment underpinned many other endeavours.

I was very broadly trained in 'general' surgery, and operated on every part of the intestinal tract from oesophagus to anus. Only latterly did gut surgery become subspecialised.

I treated many patients. They were major cases, and each time I saw somebody, usually in clinic, I would remember a little fact about them. That made the interaction more human at such a worrying time. Good ice breakers were the footy, and for persons from the South Coast, the Port Elliot bakery!

The most efficient operations on patients were achieved when a team of experienced individuals was formed. This could be in clinics or endoscopy, but was most developed in the operating theatres. With a skilled anaesthetist, theatre nurse and assistant, one could get through a lot of work in an unhurried fashion. I recall doing just this on one day when I completed an oesophagectomy, low anterior resection and removal of a giant spleen in good time.

I made a practice of ringing a patient's relatives after an operation. There was always someone on the end of the phone who was most grateful for the call. I emphasised this to my registrars. This simple extension of humanity had a remarkably positive impact. We never touted for gifts, but there were some, and the best were cards of thanks. It takes a heart-felt effort to write something. I have two files full of such cards.

I ran an audit of our Unit's results for cancer surgery over 10 years. This database was set up by **Dr Rajeev Kapoor**, who was our Fellow from the Christian Medical College (CMC) at Ludhiana in India. I checked all the data, before it was entered in the Cancer Registry by **Lesley Milliken**. Links to Births, Deaths and Marriages had been set up by **Dr David Roder**, with whom I collaborated on a number of projects, this enabled accurate mortality data to be gathered. Dr Roder worked with **Dr Colin Luke**, who understood the database and statistics. Again, you have to start somewhere, and time passes quickly. After 10 years, **Dr Steven Due** (one of our students) performed a comprehensive analysis of our data. It was found that our survival rate was preeminent in the country - and Australia ranks as one of the best in the world.

I analysed my own patients as a subset. Five-year survival is the magic time for bowel cancer beyond which recurrence is rare. If you walked through my door in clinic, the chance of you being alive in five years from that time was 79.5%!

All this was done gratis. Eventually matters were tightened up at the Cancer Registry, and they kept the database no more. By this time national data collection had started, the BiNational Colorectal Cancer Audit (BCCA), largely through the drive and persistence of **Dr Andrew Hunter** from the RAH.

Maybe because of my practice, I ended up often advising on surgery and home TPN cases. These were accumulated by **Dr Andrew Holt**, a talented intensive care physician. The cases came from across the State. They were all different, and it took some investigating and sorting.

Periodically, we had spectacular saves by providing surgery on these cases, even getting patients off home TPN on occasion. In other cases, the quality of life was improved with stoma revisions, and so on.

Trauma cases tend to stick in my mind. Generally, there were good outcomes, but not always. One day a young woman arrived having been severely hurt in a car accident. She had head, chest and abdominal injuries. I removed her shattered spleen for bleeding, but blood kept pouring out through the chest drain so I had to take her to theatre myself. Fortunately, I had some experience with chest work. The anaesthetist of the day was a senior practitioner who placed a double lumen tube in like a walk in the park! You should never under-estimate your colleagues. The lung was torn and the bleeding was not stopped by suturing. The only practical thing to do was to remove the lung. I had trouble controlling the lung hilum, but we managed to get her off the table and arrested the haemorrhage. Sadly, all did not work out well and she died from her other injuries.

Another sobering case was one of severe liver trauma. It was a Saturday afternoon and a young motorcyclist had hit a tree. He had many injuries and abdominal bleeding was one of them, necessitating a laparotomy. By this time, I had become familiar with the abdominal Rochard retractor, which gives excellent exposure of the upper abdomen. We found a shattered liver but were able to isolate it. A very able liver surgeon, **John Chen**, arrived and helped to complete the hemi hepatectomy, which exposed a long tear in the inferior vena cava, which we sutured. One almost never saves a patient with these injuries, and I was rather pleased when I left the staff to tidy up, only to be informed later that when he was warmed up, he suffered a cardiac arrest and could not be resuscitated. It was a devastating end.

There were 'saves' too. One was a young man with severe injuries who had been retrieved from the southeast of the State. It was a foggy night in winter and planes couldn't fly, so he came by road. When he arrived, he was as white as a sheet, but alive. He had various gut injuries, but his liver looked like marble, and a biopsy showed only a few viable hepatocytes (liver cells). He was dialysed throughout this period, to support the liver. Happily, the liver recovered, and quite some time later I closed his stomas and he appeared to suffer no ill consequence.

Another story concerned a character who assaulted the police. He kept coming at them with a machete, even after a Taser, so he was shot. The bullet took the top off of a Meckel's diverticulum (a fine and disabling shot), and exited via the right pelvis, smashing the bone. That sure stopped him.

Often the trauma cases were not very savoury at all. Once a chap was shot in the abdomen by his brother, in a drug deal. He arrived from the South Coast quite exsanguinated and with an entry wound on the front of the belly and exit wound on the back. That was not good. In short, there was a big retroperitoneal haematoma that gushed blood on opening, so I quickly clamped the aorta and then sewed up a hole in the external iliac artery. Feeling a bit proud of myself, I let the clamp off, but blood poured out the back wound in the artery. Oh well, I fixed it up, repaired the damaged intestine, and he lived to tell another day.

Another case had severe abdominal trauma with marked blood loss. We attended to the damage and arrested the haemorrhage. The Hb was 4 g/dl, a level which is not survivable without transfusion (normal is about 140 g/dl in a man). Our hands were tied, however, as he was a declared Jehovah's witness. He died right there. What followed was a difficult conversation with his family.

Early in my consultant life, I had several cases of pancreatic trauma whereby the pancreas was divided across the body of the pancreas, where it crosses the spine and aorta. This was caused by seatbelt trauma. The solution was to do a distal pancreatectomy, there was plenty of reserve for digestion and insulin production in the remainder of the pancreas. Sometimes this was possible to accomplish while preserving the splenic vessels, which are intimately attached to the back of the pancreas. One young woman was very upset about the resultant scar. She was seen by one of our pragmatic English registrars, who just looked quizzically at her and said, "Madam, you're lucky to be alive!"

A terrible and distressing case that I'm sure is burned in everyone's memory was that of a young man retrieved from a building site where a large concrete block had fallen on him. He had already had several cardiac arrests before reaching hospital. I ended up opening his chest in an attempt to control the bleeding, but to no avail, and he died. Counsellors were brought in for all the staff, but they couldn't possibly undo the trauma of such an experience.

In later years, when a patient died for whatever reason I wrote to the relatives of that person. This seemed like a human thing to do. I have only encountered one other doctor who did the same. He is a senior surgeon from Melbourne, who obviously has a large measure of humanity. That same person, **Ian Jones** from RMH, rang me one day to thank me for my involvement in the 'Research Committee of the Colorectal Surgical Society of Australia and New Zealand' that shows a fine sense of correctness, if not gratitude.

A surgery that I will never forget was that of a young woman with a severely damaged oesophagus and stomach, due to caustic soda ingestion. It eventually came to resection to remove the damaged gullet. I had done a number of oesophagectomies by the transhiatal approach and was doing this case that way, till I encountered a solid block of tissue high up in the mediastinum. This came away and the anaesthetist suddenly reported no airway and no blood pressure! I was momentarily paralysed. Luckily, my experienced SR of the day, Rajeev Kapoor, said, "We need to open the chest." This we did by turning the patient on her right side (up), and we found a torn azygous vein and membranous trachea. I'd had the foresight to warn a cardio thoracic surgery colleague, **Dr John Knight**, that he may be required and he came and repaired the damage. I had to complete the operation - after a cup of tea!

On another occasion I had a call from my SR, **Dr Scott Mansfield**, about a patient in extremis from gut bleeding one week after a Whipple's procedure, a large pancreas operation. It was 7.00am and the original team could not be found. We took her to theatre. The situation was complex and it took a while to define the anatomy. She kept bleeding, and at times her blood pressure sagged to 0. Dr Mansfield was a well-built Queenslander and every so often he was doing cardiac massage. A blood pressure monitor (arterial line) showed that he was quite effective. With chest compressions there is often the horrible sensation of fracturing ribs and sternum in the older patient. Eventually, the situation was controlled. I went to see the patient later, to check on her progress. She was blissfully unaware of the drama and said, "I have a terrible pain in my chest, doctor."

Gaining experience in vascular surgery and dealing with large blood vessels was valuable. Sometimes, this involved exposing the superior mesenteric artery, just below the transverse colon to either retrieve a blood clot from atrial fibrillation or to bypass a blockage, with help from vascular colleagues. It was not easy to diagnose mesenteric ischaemia, and my registrar of the day summarised a series of cases as, "the good, the bad and the ugly".

It pays to be aware of the lessons of medical history. It was infrequent but I did encounter situations where wounds/anastomoses would not heal despite standard measures. I eventually twigged to the fact that the patients were deficient in Vitamin C – that is, they had scurvy! This problem was prevalent in ancient sailors and was eventually solved by Scottish doctor, James Lind. Dr Lind did what is portrayed to be the first clinical trial in medicine, he gave one group of sailors fresh fruit and the other did not receive any. The first group had a marked reduction in scurvy.

The first such case I recall was a rather overweight woman from a country town. We found she was stashing her fruit and vegetables in the fridge. She simply wouldn't eat them. We eventually gave her Vit C parenterally, and she healed up. Another even more puzzling case was a vegan whose Vit C levels were very low. Oral Vit C corrected the problem. She wrote a grateful letter of thanks, which acknowledged the personal care she received.

Some rare events occurred. One patient with a diverticular perforation had Ehlers-Danlos syndrome, which is a rare connective tissue problem. He had the full range of problems, including aortic replacement and cataracts. He came to me for reversal of his stoma, and at laparotomy I picked up the small bowel and it fell to pieces! Needless to say, the re-anastomosis was watched very carefully. Fortunately, all was well.

I have detailed the case of a phaeochromocytoma nestled between the cava and aorta. I was involved in other difficult phaeos. One was a recurrent malignant phaeo. I was 'assisting' a fellow surgeon and took the mass off the left diaphragm after reflecting the spleen and tail of pancreas. On another occasion, a MIBG scan had shown a second phaeo, they can be multiple, sitting on the right crus, the muscle to the diaphragm. This was neither in the chest nor the abdomen and the patient was a hefty man. It was sitting on the aorta where it runs through the diaphragm. If not for the fancy scan, we would never have known about it. Finally, I was involved in a recurrent phaeo, recurrent high blood pressure, that involved clearing along the aorta and removing the left kidney, which Dr Mark Siddins did.

I performed quite a few traumatic splenectomies. Occasionally the splenic capsule was torn during colectomy and the bleeding could not be stopped, so it had to be removed. The patients all received immunisations postop, to reduce the risk of overwhelming post-splenectomy sepsis (OPSI). I only ever saw one case of this in a splenectomised patient, and that patient died. There was a vogue for preserving the spleen, but I never did this if the spleen was too badly damaged. The joke went around that 'the best way of preserving the spleen is in formalin'.

I recall a young woman for whom we were removing recurrent ovarian cancer, including a pelvic mass. Upon removal, she promptly had cardiac arrest, perhaps due to a pulmonary embolism. It required a taxing phone call, followed by an interview. This was somewhat redolent of speaking to the relatives of the young man who had died of severe trauma, but had refused blood transfusion as he was a Jehovah's Witness.

I was sent difficult cases of constipation and because I ran the anorectal studies lab, I was sent some cases of adult Hirschsprung's disease. That is where there are absent ganglion cells in the distal bowel and therefore, disturbed motility. This is a congenital malformation and usually the newborn has a bowel obstruction. When the segment is short, they can struggle through to adult life. The condition is diagnosed by an absent anorectal reflex and a biopsy of the distal rectum. Treatment was an internal anal sphincterectomy, as taught to me by a paediatric surgeon. This resolved the symptoms in some cases.

In others, there was no effect however, as there was a megacolon (enlarged) that did not improve. The solution was to resect the colon and rectum and fashion an ileoanal pouch. This was rather worrying, having divided the internal anal sphincter before. I consulted a surgeon in Queensland, an ex-President of the RACS, regarding such a case. He responded that if the patient was a man, all was likely to be okay. He was right, the patient only had faecal leakage when hoisting up a big truck tyre!

Other tough cases were necrotising fasciitis affecting the perineum. Wide debridement was the rule, and it often involved stoma formation, as the perineum was raw. I will never forget a young woman with meningococcal disease. I have never seen such an ill patient who was still alive. The only area of uninvolved skin was the left lower quadrant, and that is where we had to place a colostomy. I understand she survived and is now well and stoma-free.

I have seen a plastic surgeon repairing the brachial plexus and doing muscle transfers to improve function. It was on a Saturday, and as I was at the hospital, I dropped in to see a wonderful anatomical dissection of that complicated plexus. I only ever knew that anatomy for the exams, the surgeon was **Dr Philip Griffen**.

An interesting patient was in severe abdominal pain, but we couldn't find a cause. Eventually, a repeated rectal biopsy diagnosed ischaemic changes in the rectum, and an arteriogram showed a narrowed inferior mesenteric artery. Remarkably, a vascular stent was inserted but improvement was only brief and he came to have a resection of the left colon and rectum. The pathologist diagnosed amyloidosis affecting the vessels and his pain was relieved. One should never give up.

One Saturday, we had our girls at netball when I received a call from an ophthalmologist. He was requesting a neck node biopsy, on himself. He had diagnosed lung cancer himself and had an enlarged node. I knew the patient well, he was a brilliant doctor and researcher. The node was sitting on the phrenic nerve. While I was operating, it was an exercise in anatomy. The human being emerged afterwards.

One unusual gift was a hunting knife from an American patient. The knife was Davy Crockett-style and rather lethal. I had another patient with a large bowel tumour invading the stomach, which had been bypassed by an American surgeon. I was able to remove the tumour and part of the stomach. I received a nice letter from the surgeon concerned. In another instance, a patient had a physician friend in New York. She was a complex patient metabolically and she wrote to her friend overseas. I had been expecting criticism from that doctor, but received a pleasant correspondence.

A notable world event I can relate to my surgical lists, was when the Twin Tower bombings occurred in New York. I had commenced a case of bowel cancer, in an older man with a young wife and children when I heard murmurings amongst the staff. After the procedure was concluded, I went to the tea room and there was absolute silence as everyone was transfixed by the unfolding events on the TV. I remember when Princess Diana lost her life in Paris. We were on holiday in Queensland and Margaret was asleep. It was mid-afternoon and the football broadcast was interrupted, it had to be important to pause the football. Her injuries were rather similar to my patient with the torn lung. Everyone places times and events when these occurred.

Patients generally followed advice, but not always. One such case presented with a de novo small bowel obstruction proven to be a tumour at the end of the small intestine. The obstruction resolved and curative surgery was recommended, but the patient refused. I saw him over time, and he eventually developed metastases and the carcinoid syndrome. It was such a shame, as he could have been cured by surgery.

I had similar severe cases in the Flinders Private Hospital and infrequently, I would transport patients across to the theatres at FMC as they were always available. From there it would be back to ICU in FPH, where the staff were the same. This caused some consternation with FPH administrators but they didn't argue with having the patient's best interests at heart.

The toughest patients on the planet are not husky soldiers but little old ladies. They have generally seen out a war or two, had a gaggle of kids, and they were usually up making the bed the day after major surgery.

There is an amusing aphorism, "If you don't eat, you don't shit. If you don't shit, you die." That summarises gastrointestinal surgery.

Lessons:

Patients are the focus of all our endeavours.
There are highs and lows.
Be competent, but above all, be kind.

Chapter 29

Nursing Staff and Allied Health

The real hour-to-hour work of looking after the patients was done by a legion of nursing staff, too numerous to mention. Doctors come and go, and leave instructions which are enacted by the nursing staff, from charting of observations and fluid balance, administering drugs and providing emotional support to persons at very vulnerable times in their lives.

Of the numerous excellent ward nurses with whom I have worked, two particular groups of skilled nurses stand out. The first of these are the theatre nurses. Not much would happen without their organisation in the operating theatre. They are highly skilled, highly trained and just generally good persons with whom to work, either for a regular operating list or emergency situations.

The nurses are great gossips. They were on my case for ages to get married. At our wedding ceremony they sent a message which was read out. Next, it was on to, "When are you going to have children?" After we had a daughter it was, "When are you having another?"

I have listed just some of these wonderful nurses in the Appendix, and their names are shown under their photo in this chapter.

The second group is the stomal therapists. These nurses are specialised in the care of patients with stomas, where the bowel is brought to the surface; or it might be a urinary stoma, or problematic wound. This is an enormously confronting situation for the patient and it takes much training and skill to deal with a stoma, both physically and emotionally. Erica Taylor, Bronwyn Bolto and Paula Moran come to mind.

It was so important to have a positive attitude with the patients. One particular nurse worked in the Oncology Unit delivering chemotherapy to the sickest of patients, and her wonderful attitude had a profound impact on them. **Joyce McLean** was her name, and she hailed from Scotland.

The much-understated role of the physiotherapists, social workers, dieticians and occupational therapists needs to be recorded here. Indeed, the notes from physiotherapy are more complete than the medical notes in many cases!

At the end of my time, I took all the nurses out to lunch at the restaurant at Serafino Wines, McLaren Vale. That's just me and 20 women! It may sound like nirvana, but 20 theatre nurses talk a lot and they make a fair amount of noise!

Lesson:

Value your colleagues in nursing and allied health, and take the time to thank them.

Theatre nurses - lunch at Serafino's, McLaren Vale.

Back: *Jess Fawcett, Carla Iveson, Lea West, Jennie Polis, Cath Coombe, Carol Kirby, Lisa Oliver, Lyndal Klei, Ali Horner, Sally Paneros, Annie Richardson.*

Front: *Terri Delaine, myself, Sue Wager, Gill Sims.*

Nurses and colleagues at FPH, at my retirement.

Front row: *Anu Baby, Emily Drechsler, Emily Benham, Ruth Langton, Mini Cherian, Bindu Varghese, Charlotte Bayre, Hong Mao*

2nd row: *Antony Kaithathara, Paula Moran, Paul Griffiths, Bron Bolto, Toni Pitt, Sharon Griffiths, Julia Ferguson, Manjula Johnson, Claire McCaffery, Patricia Finlay, Liah Harding.*

3rd row: *Rheena Thangavelu, Joady Cooper, Sheena Mitchell, Kerri Haskett, Matt Schwerna, Dr Eaton, Luigi Sposato, Darren Mounkley, Dayan DeFontagalland, T Sia.*

Very back: *Dr Siddins and Faith Siddins*

Chapter 30

Meetings

Attending and presenting at meetings is a big part of academic life. A benefit is that you get to meet up with colleagues.

There were some very interesting experiences, among them:

- I was the key organiser for a meeting of the 'Surgical Research Society'. It was being held at FMC. Our first child had been born in the early hours the preceding day! First, there was a complaint that the coffee was cold. Second, a character was fuming, as he had walked all the way from the accommodation at Glenelg despite numerous notices about buses. I didn't find any of this funny at the time.
- Donald Beard (senior surgeon) gave us various entertaining tutorials, including first-hand accounts of the doctors who dealt with the shootings of Pope John Paul 2 and Ronald Reagan. On one occasion when he was giving a talk, a younger colleague had his children there. They were making

a bit of noise, as youngsters do, and the man made moves to exit with his children. Don Beard merely said, "Don't take them out - it will reduce the audience numbers!"

- I presented the results of innervation of the human oesophagus at the local surgeons' meeting, and was awarded the RP Jepson Medal for the work.

- At the 'Digestive Disease Week' in San Francisco, USA, there were memorable social events. I recollect that they served strawberries with cream prior to a trip to see a Monet Exhibition. That was probably organised by a drug company and would now be viewed as unethical.

- At the annual conference of the RACS there is often a guest speaker from outside the profession. One year, the meeting was at Wrest Point in Hobart, and the speaker was Sir Edmund Hillary. By great chance, I had purchased a copy of his biography that very morning and wanted to get his signature. I was somewhat overawed by the great man and hung around in the background. As I was circulating around, after his lecture, hoping to get his autograph in the book, one of our SA surgeons, Donald Beard (aka 'the colonel') spotted me and went straight up to Sir Ed and said, "This young man wants you to sign your book." So, I have an autographed copy of Sir Edmund Hillary's biography.

- I obtained the signature of Mark Killingback, a doyen of Australian bowel surgery, in his book *Colorectal Surgery*.

- For some reason I was asked to give a talk on massive transfusion at the CSSANZ meeting in Victor Harbour – hopefully I wasn't deemed an expert in this area.

- I co-chaired a session on surgery in home TPN cases, with a visiting expert from the UK. His experience dwarfed mine.

- I presented our work on lower gastrointestinal bleeding cases at a 'Quality' meeting. It was well received, and I deferred the initiative to Dr Padbury.

- I had learned to film open operations with a laparoscope as it provided a much closer view. At a national meeting, I presented how I dissected the splenic flexure of the colon. I would start all left-sided dissections by opening the lesser sac, freeing the flexure and ligating the IMV, then IMA high. I thought it was a nice video. My presentation was followed by a Queensland surgeon doing a laparoscopic case, so my presentation was rather overshadowed.

Lessons:

Learn from others.
Presenting at meetings is not easy.

Chapter 31

Arts in Health

This unique venture came about when the artist **Avril Thomas** was employed to come to the operating theatres and capture the action. I feel that a painting brings much more life to a subject than a photograph. The project came under the overall umbrella of 'Arts in Health', and was led by **Sally Thomas**. The CSPF recognised and supported these endeavours.

Many of the surgeons of the day were painted while they were at work. A particular favourite for me was the painting of **Dr Bob Foreman**, a somewhat iconoclastic vascular surgeon, crouched over the arm of a patient in which he is constructing an arteriovenous fistula for dialysis.

When the display was opened by the Minister for Health, John Hill, I gave a speech on the significance of these works. Some of the paintings were purchased by our own Department and hang in the Department of Surgery

Years later, I commissioned the same artist to do a series of paintings of me in the theatre, operating. Contrary to popular belief, surgeons by and large are self-conscious folk. While I felt strange embarking on this venture, the paintings capture perfectly what I have spent much of my working life doing.

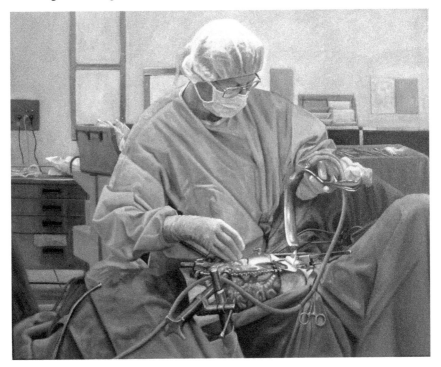

Painting of David Wattchow operating. Artist Avril Thomas

To Dave,

It has been a pleasure to work with you — one of the best surgeons I have worked with (and I've worked with a lot!) Hope you enjoy this bit of light reading

Graeme McLeay

[signature]

8 · 8 · 10

Dear David,
With grateful thanks for
your supurb craftmanship
and genuine compassion
during my recent illness
with best wish and
good walking

Some gratifying comments from patients and colleagues

Lesson:

It is important to have some colour in your life!

Chapter 32

A Bit of Fun

My work journey sounds like a lot of hard effort, but there were some fun times too. Most notable was the 'Flinders Amateur Revue and Theatrical Society' (FARTS). It was a group of disparate persons from throughout the Medical Centre. They put on an annual review that had many good skits, probably the best was 'The Dancing Professors' dressed as babies. Equally good was when **Rosemary Wilde**, Secretary to the Professor of Surgery, and **John Turnidge**, Microbiologist, were sparking off each other. Sadly, the Revues do not happen anymore, as everyone is too busy.

There were cricket games too, these still happen. The matches are staff versus students, and usually the staff have the upper hand. I remember **John Chalmers** (Professor of Medicine), and **Ray Yates** (Senior Animal House officer) going out to bat. Ray had set up an excellent animal house and facility and oversaw it for many years. While I was a PhD student, I did some surgery on a dog in the animal house. The dog had a small bowel fistula created, and I reversed the fistula to make the animal's final days easier.

There was an active staff society, of which I was the Treasurer. A principal function of the society was to champion the causes of the medical staff, but we arranged various dinners that were well attended.

'The Dancing Professors'- Jones, Watts, Kalucy, Kneebone, Radford

Prof Geffen hamming it up.

Cricket games – 'The Flannelled Fools', John Chalmers and Ray Yates going out to bat; Jack Alpers, fast bowler.

Chapter 33

Alumni

Flinders Medical graduates have a very strong affinity for their university and hospital and teachers.

An early Alumni Committee.

L to R: *Bob Ayres, Michael Harry (Secretary), Nick Twidale, Trevor Collinson, Jack Wearne, Jeff Bowden, Neil Jones, John Brayley, Gillian Marshmann.*

Nowadays, one hears of few alumni gatherings, although perhaps a main residual function is the awarding of an annual prize from old Alumni. This prize was created for graduates who contributed substantially outside medicine. I am constantly amazed at the endeavours of the current students.

Forty years after our enrolment, there was a university-wide celebration at the Festival Centre and a 'medical' gathering at the Town Hall. A chief highlight of the gathering was a performance by the band 'Redgum'. The lead singer, John Schumann, an Arts graduate of Flinders University, gave a heartfelt rendition of the song *I Was Only 19*. The song pertains to the Vietnam War, which was in our time.

At another get together at the Adelaide Town Hall, we were riveted by an interview by Dr Karl Kruszelnicki of Dr Richard Harris, who was involved in the Thailand cave rescue (Dr Harris is a Flinders alumnus).

The functioning of the Alumni was supported by the University. **Callista Thillou, Jane Russell** and **Bonnie Allmond** were key advocates for the medical alumni. It was, and is, a different 'corporate' world.

Lesson:

Remember your roots and give something back.

Chapter 34

Philanthropy

There is a very strong tradition in North America whereby doctors donate, often substantially, to their alma mater. I have observed that it is often commemorated with a plaque or notice at a laboratory or elsewhere. We do not have such a strong tradition in Australia, I think that we could take a leaf from the North Americans here.

I always considered I was well paid for my work at FMC. When I started treating private patients, I would never charge more than either Medicare or what the health funds allowed. I did not need to advertise, patients came my way. It soon became evident that I could earn a considerable amount of money and I chose to put my earnings from private patients into a trust fund.

Gus Fraenkel was fond of saying, "The best philanthropy is guided by enlightened self-interest." I followed this principle in directing my monies to the areas of neuroscience and surgery. My earliest donation was to the 'Sir Mark Oliphant Fund', which was set up to support research endeavours at FMC. I have a fancy certificate marking this contribution. There was a notice board related to this on Level 2, but it has now disappeared.

I have been able to support areas of interest to me, primarily our collaborative effort with the scientists of the Human Physiology group. I had to apply for the use of those funds and go through a legitimate process. This was largely through the CSPF, which approved use of those monies.

In brief, the funds were used to create PhD scholarships and employ scientists. They were key to the provision of a salary for **Dr Dinning**, a hospital scientist, until a full appointment was gained. It seems extraordinary that I could make this money doing what I was trained to do, but could not get grants from the NHMRC. Still, a dollar is a dollar. I even supported the Divisional Convocation on two occasions, along with student requests for travel.

The arrangements for full-time staff were helpful. Under our award we were allowed to use the consulting facilities of the Flinders Medical Centre, and the staff were very helpful. We could spend a session (a half day) a week outside the hospital, and I eventually rolled this into a full day's operating per fortnight at Flinders Private Hospital. There were good arrangements for billings and indemnity too.

A valuable vehicle was set up by the University to disburse donated funds. It bears the name of the first Vice-Chancellor of Flinders University, 'The Karmel Endowment Fund'. As a result of this, I had a meeting with the then Dean, Paul Worley, and then Vice-Chancellor, Michael Barber.

Once I had earned enough funds, I set about establishing a PhD scholarship relating to the lab and surgery. Over the years, this meant I have been able to support a number of PhD students, largely in surgery but in science too. As this was done via the mechanism of the 'Clinicians' Special Purpose Fund', which was where most of the private practice money was banked, I had to apply for each scholarship and satisfy the Committee that the money would be well spent.

I did 20 years of private practice and was quite busy, so I generated good funds. In the last few years, Simon Brookes drew my attention to the work of Phil Dinning on new ways of recording bowel motility, which were revolutionising these recordings. Dr Dinning and his colleague, John Arkwright, were awarded the 'Eureka Prize' in science for this discovery. As it happened, Dr Dinning finished up as a scientist in NSW. With the help of Nick Spencer, we were able to attract him to come and work with our group. Some hard cash was needed, and I had $200,000 available from earnings and was able to use this for his salary. Senior scientists don't come cheap, the annual salary was $100,000, but with the collaboration of our science group, a series of ground-breaking experiments were achieved.

Importantly, I helped to fund some scientists who were working with Simon Brookes on understanding the actions on the gut of the laxative Bisacodyl. I established the 'Neuro-Gastroenterology and Motility Fund' with the help of Simon Brookes and Flinders University. This was a subsidiary of the Karmel Fund. This fund underwrites activities in the lab, and still operates. The transfer of money from the hospital to university setting was aided by **Di Holmes** and **Cobus Lotheringen** in Administration.

At the end of my time in private practice, I found that I had donated over $2 million to research in its various forms. In my view, this is right and ethical, and one can only set an example.

Recently, Margaret and I donated $10,000 to support a travel fund for neuroscience. That was an expensive cup of tea at the University! I also donated my surgical and anatomical texts to the 'Yungorrendi First Nations Centre for Higher Education and Research' at Flinders University.

Clinician establishes Phd scholarship in his field

As far as David Wattchow is concerned, it is important for clinicians to have an affiliation with scientists.

"We see clinical problems everyday that could be improved, and they are able to improve things through scientific investigation," Associate Professor Wattchow, who is the Director of Gastrointestinal Surgery at Flinders Medical Centre, said.

To that end, Associate Professor Wattchow has earmarked some of his earnings to go towards a scholarship for a PhD in gut neuroscience as problems with bowel function are very common in clinical practice, and after operations on the gastrointestinal tract.

As a clinician at FMC, Associate Professor Wattchow is allowed to earn a certain amount in private practice but any excess is deposited into the Clinicians' Special Purpose Fund, which supports research and other educational activities.

The fund, of which Associate Professor Wattchow is the chair of trustees - who include Dr Robert Bryce, Dr Geoffrey Bowden, Dr Andrew Holt, Dr Jane Wood and Mr Gary Verstegen - supports a number of philanthropic activities, including funding scholarships, conferences and individuals.

Professor David Wattchow: creating a PhD Scholarship in gut neuroscience

For example, it has for a number of years funded a $30,000 NHMRC level scholarship for a medical PhD student, and has recently agreed to fund graduate Dr Luke Johnson to present papers on his experience working in the aftermath of the Asian tsunami at a conference in Europe.

Associate Professor Wattchow, himself a graduate in 1980 of the first intake of Flinders Medical School, has opted to earmark his contribution to the fund to set up the $140,000 four-year scholarship. This follows on from a previous donation

of $90,000 in 2003 that funded a PhD scholarship for a surgeon in training, Dr Dayan DeFontgalland.

He said he had decided on a gut neuroscience scholarship as it was an area of interest to him. There has been a long and productive collaboration between the Departments of Surgery (with Professors Marcello Costa and Simon Brookes) and Physiology in this regard resulting in no less than five surgical PhDs.

" I think if you ask people just to donate it can get a bit nebulous," he said.

"This might be a way of encouraging clinicians to support an endeavour in an area that they know is a clinical problem.

"Creating a PhD scholarship in an area of interest with the University is a way of clinicians supporting the development of clinician/scientists for the future, and the university has the administrative capability to manage scholarships."

It is expected that the scholarship will be up and running for the 2008 academic year.

Associate Professor Wattchow's scholarship is just one of many funded by benefactors of the University.

For more information contact Lauran Huefner in the Development Office on 8201 2673. ■

Philanthropy is important.

Lesson

You will have a good income, and you can afford to share it round.

Chapter 35

Companion of the University and AM

To my great surprise, I was offered several accolades at the end of my career. I was made a 'Companion of the University' in 2016. This is a rare honour, and I was the first member of the School of Medicine, as it was then, to be accorded it. I imagine that the Dean, Paul Worley, had something to do with it all, but a suitable committee had vetted the nomination. The occasion involved donning some ornate robes and a floppy hat and receiving the honour at a Graduation Ceremony, at which I gave a short speech. I was able to use those robes again at a subsequent Graduation Ceremony for our PhD students.

In 2017, I was even more surprised to receive a letter from the Governor-General, on very ornate parchment, informing me that I had been nominated to be made a 'Member of the Order of Australia'(AM). I cannot uncover who made this nomination as one is not to be informed, but I do know the office of the Governor-General rang various persons to check my bona fides.

Months went by and finally the letter of offer arrived. This I accepted mostly I felt, because it was on behalf of other persons – my wife, family, and all the wider group of people who had supported me. A ceremony was held in Government House at which the South Australian Governor, Mr Hui van Le, AC pinned the medal on my chest. It was possibly the only time I would get a free park in Government House! Pomp and ceremony have its place.

Lesson:

These honours come along if you go over and above your job.

David Wattchow and Simon Brookes at the award ceremony for the 'Companion of the University', 2016

Dr Hains presenting the honour.

Receiving the AM, from the Governor of South Australia, Mr Hui van Le, AC

Chapter 36

Family and a Life Outside Medicine

It may seem odd to place family support at the end of such a dissertation as this, rather than first. The backing from my family has been the most important factor in my long career. I simply could not have done all this without the love and support of my wife, Margaret. We met in the 'Adelaide Bushwalkers', but had much more in common than bushwalking.

Having interests outside medicine is very important, and this is recognised by the 'Alumni Prize'. My colleagues have done all sorts of things, including sport at high levels, music, family.

In my own case, I joined the 'Adelaide Bushwalkers' while still a medical student. This was an eclectic group of characters who had virtually nothing to do with the world of medicine. It gradually opened up travel and exploration for me, and led to a modicum of independence in terms of survival.

Margaret and I have undertaken various challenging walks in the Adelaide Hills and Flinders Ranges, in the Grampians in Victoria, and further afield in other States of Australia. Tasmania being a particular favourite. I have undertaken journeys throughout that State, including the Franklin River shortly after it was saved from being dammed, and the Arthur Range in the South West.

We have gone on to pursue other activities such as rock climbing (Morialta and Hills, Arapiles and Flinders), cross country skiing, cycle touring and canoeing. Although South Australia is the driest state in Australia, there are lovely backwaters on the River Murray to explore. We particularly like loading up our Canadian canoe with gear, and heading off.

With a long-term purpose to collect available wood supplies, there was a humorous incident when I was unloading big logs from the back of the car and one rolled out onto my foot. Ouch. I kept on unloading, but eventually noticed blood oozing from my shoe. Closer inspection showed my left great toe was lacerated, I bound it up, put a sandal on, and carried on. The following afternoon, it was still bleeding despite the pressure. I was at home and had a telephone call, regarding a medical situation, followed by a visit from SA Police regarding the sudden tragic death at home of a young patient who had advanced bowel cancer. The police officers came into our home to find me with my leg up and blood-soaked bandages on my foot. Needless to say, the terminal phalanx was shattered, and later that evening I had surgery to piece it all together. I'm sure Margaret breathed a sigh of relief that I was confined to hospital for a couple of days!

We dealt with various childhood maladies. Suffice it to say both daughters survived and have gone on to valuable professional careers.

The greatest thing to come from joining the bush walking club was falling in love with my life partner, Margaret, and all that has flowed from there.

Lesson:

There is a full life to lead. Live it.

My wife Margaret, with me.

Our daughters Naomi (right) and Kimberley (left) at Barwon Heads, Victoria.

Chapter 37

Conclusions

In this book, I have focused on the development of the Flinders Medical School and Centre, which has had an enormous influence on me personally and professionally. My time there was indeed special.

The establishment of the school has attracted many dedicated and intelligent persons from throughout the globe. Their teaching and enthusiasm have created a valuable legacy for all and led to many of the students branching out all over the world.

All of the young graduates from the first intake grew up to contribute to society in many ways. Matthew Flinders and Gus Fraenkel would be proud.

Sculpture outside Physical Sciences building at Flinders University

Appendix

Theatre nurses at FMC I have known and with whom I have worked:

Lea West: A Senior Nurse who became the architect of the new operating theatres which were foreshadowed by a report by John Menadue.

Jennie Polis: A Senior Nurse, who had worked in all disciplines, and a very elegant lady.

Carol Kirby: A Senior Nurse who became a Coordinator of the theatres, including emergencies.

Annie Richardson: A nurse who was involved from the early days of liver transplantation and other major surgery.

Sue Wager: A nurse who worked on my list for ages.

Lisa Oliver: A salt of the earth nurse. Lisa and family, along with mine, were famously camped in Parachilna Gorge in the Flinders Ranges when there was a downpour!

Margie Stegmeyer: A Senior Nurse.

Cath Coombe: A nurse who worked everywhere, including the ED. We joked about the purulent and contaminated abdomens with which we dealt.

Lyndal Klei: A night nurse chiefly, who introduced me to the idea of the Bookwalter retractor. One can learn a lot from nurses, and I subsequently developed the use of this retractor for bowel surgery.

Gill Sims: A nurse who worked on my list for ages.

Ali Horner: A very experienced nurse who worked with Dr Neil McIntosh, the first Chief Resident.

Terri McDowell: Long-time nurse for whom apparently, I sewed up a heel laceration when I was a medical student.

Sally Paneros: My most recent Senior Nurse in theatres. Sally made sure all the Junior Nurses started with me.

Carla Iveson: The preceding main nurse involved with bowel surgery,

Jessica Fawcett: A Junior Nurse who hailed from Bendigo, started with me and soon became a Senior Nurse.

List of Acronyms

AC	Companion of Australia
AM	Member of the Order of Australia
BCCA	BiNational Colorectal Cancer Audit
ChAT	choline acetyl transferase
CAG	Clinical Advisory Group
CEO	Chief Executive Officer
CSPF	Clinicians' Special Purpose Fund
CSSANZ	Colorectal Surgical Society of Australia and New Zealand
COX	Cyclooxygenase
CT	Computerized Tomography
DNA	Deoxy Ribose Nucleic Acid
DDW	Digestive Disease Week
ED	Emergency Department
ENS	enteric nervous system
ERCP	endoscopic retrograde cholangiopancreatography
EDRF	Endothelial Derived Relaxing Factor
FMC	Flinders Medical Centre
FPH	Flinders Private Hospital
FRACP	Fellow of Royal Australasian College of Physicians
FRACS	Fellow of the Royal Australasian College of Surgeons

GAMSAT	General Australian Medical School Admissions Test
GIST	Gastrointestinal Stromal Tumours
GP	General Practitioner
GSA	General Surgeons Australia
HIV	Human Immunodeficiency Virus
kRAS	Kirsten Rat Sarcoma Virus
ICU	Intensive Care Unit
MDT	Multidisciplinary Team
MIBG	iodine-123 meta-iodobenzylguanidine
NHMRC	National Health and Medical Research Council
NEJM	New England Journal of Medicine
NOS	Nitric Oxide Synthase
OSCE	Ordered Structured Clinical Examination
PPI	Proton Pump Inhibitors
PBL	Problem-based learning
PCA	Patient Controlled Analgesia
OPSI	overwhelming post-splenectomy sepsis
RGH	Repatriation General Hospital
RAH	Royal Adelaide Hospital
RACS	Royal Australasian College of Surgeons
RMO	Resident Medical Officer
RPA(H)	Royal Prince Alfred Hospital
RPJepson	Richard Pomfreet Jepson
SA	South Australia
SAASM	South Australian Audit of Surgical Mortality
SCIM	Structured Clinical Instruction Module
SHO	Senior House Officer
SLICE	Single Larger Incision Cost-Effective Surgery
SALHN	Southern Adelaide Local Health Network
SR	Senior Registrar
TH	Tyrosine Hydroxylase
TPN	total parenteral nutrition
USA	United States of America
VC	Vice Chancellor

Ingram Content Group UK Ltd.
Milton Keynes UK
UKHW021149120323
418423UK00012B/213